The Woodlands of Ivor

By Robert La Combe

Forest Raven Press
Galax, Virginia

Contents

Introduction

The heart of a naturalist can be inspired and moved by things the average person has no awareness of. Modern people living in urban environments are perhaps dull to the sensations of the natural world.

But, take away the sounds of engines and machinery and all the noises that make up the comings and goings of mankind and there is a constant. The sounds that have been with us since the beginning of our existence as a species. Bird songs floating down from the trees, the hum of a million insects in nearby foliage, the music of water flowing and tumbling over and around rocks in water ways, the breezes coursing through pines and oaks. The many passion plays, life and death struggles, loves and losses are representative in this aria and not that much different from the same creatures that still dwell in the forests and meadow places left to them.

As with all living things, our lives concern themselves with relationships. With each other, with other species, and our environment. Our ability to understand and navigate those relationships determines our success as individuals as well as a species.

This book and the essays written therein are about those relationships.

Going Home

I've heard it said that two of the most important events in a person's life are leaving home, and going back home. Home can mean different things to different people. For some, "home" is that house they grew up in, or that town where they graduated from high school. To others, home is wherever their mother lives.

For me, "home" was ten acres of paradise nestled in the heart of farm country in Southwestern Ontario. The house was hidden from the road in a clearing in the woods. A stream ran through the back yard with a waterfall that dropped into a small pool hardly big enough to swim in. We moved there the summer I turned twelve.

The back door opened up to a world that was nothing short of glorious. Where everything begged inspection. The sights, sounds and smells intoxicated and overwhelmed my senses.

One summer morning while following the stream, I came upon an old man sitting on a rock.

We talked for a while and I learned his name was Roy Ivor: a famous ornithologist and author, who had written a book and assorted articles for National Geographic He invited me back to his house, which was little more than a small cottage in the woods surrounded by huge aviaries filled with all kinds of birds, from sparrows to eagles.

We sat on his porch and talked as wild chickadees and nuthatches landed on his arm or shoulder and made their way to his breast pocket, where he kept a treat of peanut chips for his friends. Even the odd chipmunk would gleefully dance up the old man's leg chasing away any competitors, crawl into his pocket, and totally stuff his cheeks before exiting.

Over the next few years Mr. Ivor (who was ninety years old when we met) and I became close.

Every day I would make my way across the meadow and through the woods to his bird sanctuary. And every day he taught me something new. People would send him injured or baby birds from all over Canada and the United States. Dutifully and methodically, he would tend to each one. This one had a broken wing, that one too young to be on its own. Each one with a story, each one getting the same level of care and respect.

I watched as his old weathered hands would slowly and gently pick up an injured bird and his fingers would feel for a break in the wing. Quietly talking in so soothing a tone, words that revealed such a deep understanding and compassion for the life that now rested in his care.

At times it was not possible to be in his presence and think of him as anything but a "Holy Man." Indeed, as I learned later in life from veterinarians, just how impossible it can be to set a broken wing or leg on a bird because of their hollow bones. He taught me how to set broken bones, taught me how to mix up special formulas to feed different baby birds, taught me the proper way to let an eagle rest on my arm. He gave me baby owls, hawks, and various song birds to take home and raise.

Sometimes I would deliberately miss the bus that came to the end of our long driveway and walk to Roy's on my way to school. "Aren't you supposed to be in school, boy?"

"Yeah, but I missed the bus."

"Of course you did. Well, come on over here and give me a hand with things before you go."

Not many days went by that I didn't spend at least some time with Roy. I spent so much time walking back and forth that I became intimate with the land between our properties. The stream, the meadow, the woods, and the orchard, where I watched trees that blossomed in the spring with sweet-smelling flowers turn to fruit, fall to the ground in September and rot. The next year the limb that hung low with fruit was dead. It was like a new wrinkle on a familiar face. All this was somehow important to me.

It was in the orchard one beautiful spring afternoon, when the grass was getting long and a warm breeze carried the scent of apple blossoms, that I gave my virginity to a young girl that lived in the farm across the ravine. But not my innocence.

I kept that until the summer I turned fifteen, when my father was transferred to a town in upstate New York. My innocence was torn from me, along with a menagerie of pets that had to be found homes for on short notice.

My paradise, my friend, left behind and we moved into an awful house on a busy street in a smelly factory town. A part of the country where it was not uncommon to have less than twenty sunny days over the course of a summer, where it was not uncommon to have five feet of snow fall in twenty-four hours, where it was not uncommon to feel a profound sense of loss.

I'm getting ready to go back home. Not the home in the woods in Southwestern Ontario. I've been back there. The stream is now a green way that runs through a sea of concrete. The farms sold to greedy developers who turned them into shopping centers, townhomes, and busy roads.

Mr. Ivor, whose furrowed brow hovered over countless birds, is buried in St. Peters cemetery on the hill. He died when he was ninety-nine.

But I am going back home. Home for me is a place in the woods. Where the breeze whispering through pine trees is the sound of my traffic, and the songs of the birds are the voices of my neighbors. Where I can once again find intimacy with my Creator through His creations. This will be my new home. Maybe it will be my last.

I still think of my old home and friend often. They are cradled in the arms of my heart where my memories give them life. My mentor, Mr. Ivor. The lines on his face ran as deep as his character. If I could be the man he was to me to just one person in this life, it would be a life filled with purpose and significance. Tomorrow I leave to go back home.

Roy Ivor

Changing Waters

When I was a boy, my family lived for a time in the country. Behind our home was a stream.

It cascaded down a succession of rock shelves for perhaps two hundred feet before finally gushing over a five-foot waterfall into a small basin just big enough to swim in. Under huge overhanging hemlocks, I would sit on a slate ledge that protruded out over the water and throw small pieces of bread into the little pool. Chub and shiners darted from the shadows and attacked my offerings in a squirming mass; reflections of light from tiny scales caused flashes of brilliant silver and illuminated the chaos of their feeding frenzy like exploding sparklers.

Crayfish clambered out from under their rocks in the hopes of grabbing a stray morsel, but that seemed unlikely, as the bread disappeared when it broke the surface.

I spied on dragonfly nymphs under the water, caught one in the cup of my hands and was rewarded with a painful bite that astonished me. Once they completed their metamorphoses and were airborne, they were impossible to catch. Their eyes, like two motorcycle helmets resting on their heads, saw everything in any direction. I could not outsmart or outmaneuver them.

Bullfrogs, painted turtles, muskrats, wood ducks, kingfishers, and herons were all common residents of my stream. For one who knew where to look, mud puppies, salamanders, snapping turtles, mink, and otter could also be encountered. Lift the rock slowly and let the current take with it the silt from the disturbance and look: a newt, a crayfish, a baby snapping turtle. Small, but intricate lives who dwell in a hidden world, and for a curious boy: treasures and mysteries that enriched his youth.

The stream was called Sawmill Creek. She continued her campaign past our property through forests and meadows, whispering her salutations to Roy Ivor as she slipped around his Winding Lane bird sanctuary and then past the old monastery, before crossing under Mississauga Road and emptying herself into the Credit River. There they combined forces for another few miles before pushing their way into Lake Ontario.

After several days of rain or a spring thaw, the stream would exceed her boundaries and roar past in a rage like an avalanche of frothy chocolate milk. I would rush down to watch this side of her, rare and exciting. The sheer volume of water rumbled like constant thunder that pulsated in my chest and I relished the lusty pandemonium she created in a former place of tranquility.

Days later, when her temper subsided, I could survey the damage and look for treasure left behind in her haste.

The waterfall was a place where daydreams were formed, then floated aimlessly downstream with the current. The imagination of youth, free from the confines of real responsibility, rising and drifting with the slightest breeze, the hum of a thousand insects or the song of a wood thrush. Often, I could hear music in the cascading water splashing against rock and moss, a virtual symphony of woodwinds, string, brass, and drum.

I listen for those ancient musicians now when I'm near a stream or river. Sometimes I get distracted and can't tune into her dulcet tone, but often if I'm alone, I can close my eyes and tune out everything but the music. A breeze blowing through the trees will add harmony, and birds often contribute a chorus. Although the aria produced from rushing water over stone is more than sufficient.

Today, my wife and I walked beside Chestnut Creek and paused to listen for her song. The stream is partially frozen and the gurgling sound it made going over and under the shelves of ice crafted a composition that can be played only during the winter season. She suggested we cup our hands to our ears and when we did, the melody of cold water slapping over rock and ice was amplified and sounded like a cathedral filled with the clacking applause of hundreds.

The spring floods roar out an intense rhythmic beat, the dog days of summer bring down a languid easy love song, and when the shadows grow long after the fall equinox, she sings a soulful song of loss and hope. Her lyrics may often be influenced by my mood, but the music is always her own. Every stream, river, or spring flowing to its own tempo, crafted only by the lay of the land and the spirit musicians that inhabit her space.

Everywhere I have lived there has been a stream or a river that figured prominently in the time I spent there. Names that stimulated my imagination: the Credit River, the Saint Lawrence, the Oswego, the Saugeen, the Catawba, the Elk River and now the New River. Many hours have been spent exploring their banks, kayaking their routes, camping by and fishing their waters. I've had close relationships with all of them, but none so intimate as the one with Sawmill Creek. Perhaps it was my age that so ingrained her lessons into my spirit; perhaps it was her spirit that made that age so memorable. Walking beside her—with her—was the greatest education I could have received.

The first buck I ever encountered was resting by her banks—invisible in the tall brown grass of fall. We surprised each other and he catapulted from his bed with a terrific grunt. Long explosive leaps carried him across the meadow, white tail flashing each time his front hooves touched the earth. The experience left me breathless, awe struck. Images of his velvet rack of antlers, bulging eyes and that great thick neck still give me chills when I think of our chance meeting.

The nests of water fowl, song birds, fierce hawks, and stoic owls were many along her pathway and I checked on them all regularly. A fox den, a hollow tree with a family of raccoons, muskrat dens made from cattail, water snakes, the dark skeletal remains of long dead elm trees, their brittle branches like long withered arms reaching for salvation in puffy white clouds against a bright blue sky. And always her song as it rolled over rocks and fallen trees, providing the sound track for this impossible spectacle of perfection and paradise.

The summer I turned fifteen was spent pulling up surveyors' stakes and sitting in a tree so a construction crew couldn't cut it down. My father was transferred in the fall and we moved south to New York state before the devastation began in earnest. I went back years later to do a presentation in a school that had been built on what was once the meadow the buck ran through. Expensive homes lined streets with names like Singing Brook Lane and Rolling Meadows Drive. At lunch I went down to the stream to see if she remembered me and to hear her song. The area had been turned into a greenway with an asphalt trail that followed her meandering path. Some of her banks were lined with white rocks in a wire mesh to control erosion, and a sickly brown foam collected in little eddies created by a lethargic current.

I walked up stream in search of the waterfall. My desire was to sit on the slate ledge and share my sandwich with the fish. A bridge had been built over her for the pleasure of cyclists and pedestrians, a mansion was now looming large in the place of our home and the great hemlocks, ferns, and wild flowers that once lined her banks were mostly gone, replaced with the type of landscaping preferred by the more socially refined. The slate outcropping had long ago broken away and lay in repose under five feet of water at the base of the falls. I lifted rocks in search of the hidden lives that once so enchanted this small pool, but they were gone, the rocks now covered in a slimy algae-like growth.

I was suddenly struck with an overwhelming feeling of grief and loss and had to just sit by the falls and try to come to terms with an anger that seemed to have thoroughly permeated my soul.

But soon I began to see how this little stream had helped to shape who I had become and influenced my perception of the world and an understanding of my place in it. Slowly my anger was replaced with great waves of gratitude and love and it was only then I could hear her music.

It was strong and beautiful, a summer love song, pure and resilient, her spirit had never left and she inspired me to add to her song:

"Oh, lover of loves, with all my heart I will cradle you in the arms of my mind where once again my memories give you glorious life. I'll remember you and all you gave me.

"Our walks together, when I poured out my innermost self without ever saying a word and you were there, comforting my soul with each step. What I owe can never be paid.

"Our spirits have been forever entwined, bound together by the maker of all things who gave us to each other, but only for our allotted time."

We've both changed, she and I. She's been around for thousands of years and has seen many changes. And how many lives has she helped to mold? How many boys and girls, men and women down through the generations have been influenced by her music? I'll never know.

But how many more are still enjoying her beauty, her playful dance over rocks and under trees?

They enjoy her for who she is today, they didn't know her in days of old and have no sense of what's been lost. When people stop on the bridge, they appreciate who she is now, and what she has to offer is no less for those who know how to listen.

The Woodlands of Ivor

It's late January in the Blue Ridge mountains. Around our home the leaves that carpet the forest floor are soft and quiet from an all-night rain. I can walk almost silently through a gentle foggy mist that has enveloped the higher elevations.

A low canopy of clouds carries sound greater distances than normally allowed. Somewhere along the ridge, a pileated woodpecker hacks away at a tree. The rhythmic, steady thud sounds like a woodsman's ax. Its beat, carried along with the mist, follows the contours of the hollow until it reaches the bottom—a rare, level area where the spring flows, where the oldest trees hold the forest in a still and silent trance. Even on the bright sunny days of midsummer, light rarely finds a spot to rest on this part of the forest floor. Moss and ferns grow thick. Salamanders, box turtles, and copper head snakes are all asleep now, under winter's spell.

The magic here isn't obvious to everyone. It's why I like to come alone. Another voice would distract from my enchantment. Sometimes I'll walk a trail that parallels the stream. If I see a man fly fishing and he doesn't see me, I don't speak to him, not even a greeting. I know he isn't here to acknowledge another man's voice.

In my life I've known many such places, become intimate with true holiness. Wanderlust has forced me to move and start again. But now, I'm all in. Come what may, my purpose is to celebrate the wildness left in this diminished land.

Beyond my Window

In our bedroom there is a large window. It overlooks the vegetable garden in the front yard.

Beyond the garden is a large enclosure where four "special needs" geese spend their nights. On the other side of the driveway is a tool shed and beyond that, up the driveway a little further, I can just make out the roof line of our little chicken coop. I can't see much else as my view is obstructed by a dense growth of trees.

Our home is in the woods. My view of the world from this vantage point may seem limited.

Still, this time of year offers a little more distance, as all but the pine trees stand naked, shivering against a low angled sun. The window faces towards the east. The rising sun and the rising moon both greet us through this window and are the reason for the thick shade that is pulled down every night.

Even with the window closed and the shade drawn there is still life that comes calling. Some nights we lie awake listening to the sounds of the others we share the forest with. Screech owls and barred owls call out their territories, yipping coyotes, fighting raccoons, and the occasional hound dog on the hunt. In the spring and summer months, whip-poor-wills and a multitude of insects add their voices to the night-time aria.

In a couple of weeks, the songs of anxious birds will begin before first light. They arrive back from a long and dangerous journey to claim jurisdiction, by singing loudest and most often in the hopes of gaining the attention of a female with particularly high standards. Winters can seem long when the days are so short. But there is something to be excited about in every season.

In the mornings, when I get out of bed, I want to pull up the shade and greet the day. But I can't be too hasty. There are four pairs of eyes that have drawn a bead on that window waiting for movement. Even the dogs resting on the front porch are alert to the sound of the blind going up and start their happy dance in anticipation of following me on the morning rounds. The geese erupt all at once like hell has just broken loose, and know that soon they will be released from the confines of their nightly prison and can resume their bossy patrolling of the grounds. Even so, most mornings I can still spare a moment after the blind is raised to acknowledge the beauty surrounding us and my gratefulness for a place in it.

The next few weeks will be an exciting time as spring unfolds herself and paints brilliant new colors, conjures intoxicating aromas and saturates her time and space with the music of breezes, birds, and insects. A soundtrack for the emerging new life of her season. This is the world where I want to live. A place where every rock or rotting log I turn over disturbs a community that will never be the same. Where pulling on one thing, you find it connected to another, and ultimately, to yourself.

There is a special time every year, usually sometime around the end of May or the beginning of June. It's different from year to year and region. But I can feel its beginning even before I awake. In fact, it is what wakes me up. Something's happening. The birds' songs seem more intense, the grass and leaves are the greenest green, pollen is thick in the air, everything is peaking, spring and summer are merging. Spring is not ready to let go and summer has waited long enough. Both giving everything at once. It makes me want to run, to love, to celebrate, create . . . feel. Ten days, two weeks, I'll awake and I know it's finished. Summer has won the battle.

The days are long now but time is short. Fall will begin her campaign for dominance in due course. But nature in all her acts reflects her faith in the future. For spring, and the new life she brings, is never far and will always come.

21

Robert La Combe

Woodland Repertoire

Before it was light, turkeys were calling from the ridgetop. I lay in bed listening and imagined a big tom strutting his stuff, tail feathers fanned out, turning in circles, trying to impress a hen who was pretending not to notice. The first hint of light was not long in coming and soon other birds were awake and forming a springtime chorus. The bright, cascading melody of a male cardinal, and the primitive jungle call of a pileated woodpecker cracked open the dawn with such enthusiasm that the forest seemed to come alive all at once.

Pine warblers, blue jays, and rose-breasted grosbeak, were soon calling out the boundaries of this season's temporary domain. An ornamental sun smiling from the front wall of our home already has a nest of house wrens. The brooding mother can be seen looking out from inside the sun's mouth. Their smooth, throaty song floats by our open window and seems extremely loud for a bird only four inches long.

Crows are awake now and sound like they have already started a game of "who can be the most annoying." Of all the birds that sing in the forest on these early spring mornings, theirs is the only voice that refuses to blend in for chorus or harmony. But they are my favorite, and just like their bold, independent personalities, their song stands alone.

Pileated woodpeckers attach themselves to the sides of trees listening for insects moving under the bark. If they like what they hear they'll hack away, removing pieces of wood the size of a man's thumb. Usually, slowly and deliberately, like a man with an ax. This morning they've found a hollow tree they are really excited about. The pair has changed things up and the woods now echo with what sounds like rapid fire rounds discharged from a weapon of mass destruction.

These crow-sized woodpeckers are the largest in North America. They are loud, sassy, and very beautiful. The holes they make in trees provide homes for other birds, reptiles, and small mammals. We enjoy having them as neighbors, and it's never a secret when they're in "the hood."

Chickadees, nuthatches, and tufted titmice are the last ones to join in, but the first ones to scold outside our window if the bird feeder is empty or if the gray squirrels have taken over.

Some mornings, as many as eight squirrels scatter when I open the door. This infuriates me, because they gobble up every ounce of food and leave nothing for the intended recipients. At times, I've considered taking action against them that would not be compatible with my present "try to live in harmony with everything" attitude. But sometimes, I want to hate those little rodents, just like I do the rabbits that mow down my vegetable and flower gardens despite my best efforts and considerable investment in rabbit fencing. I am forced to remind myself that I built our home on land they already occupied. What they take from us must be considered just compensation.

Some of our neighbors haven't arrived home yet. Indigo buntings, humming birds, scarlet tanagers, Baltimore orioles; their songs are still absent from the woodland repertoire. Though not for much longer. In spring, every day has new arrivals. If they aren't coming in from the air they are coming forth from the ground. I saw a box turtle this week. Snakes will soon be active.

Lemon balm and mint are already thick in the gardens. Fruit trees have blossomed and seemed to have escaped any killing frosts. Asparagus spears are shooting up, rhubarb is ready to harvest, raspberry canes are leafing out. Every morning the forest and our gardens have something new to show us, to teach us.

In the mountains spring arrives late. A forty-minute drive down to lower elevations and spring is two weeks ahead of where we are.

Everything is in full bloom. Even the oak trees have buds leafing out. Up here, we're just getting started.

Mourning doves coo softly from trees that tower over our home, coaxing me to fall back into a light slumber. A gentle breeze whispers through the pines, but far off a rolling thunder threatens the forest's calm. The wait has been too long—at least it feels that way—since we were able to sleep and wake with our window open. Winters are too cold; summers are often too hot. Spring and fall are the seasons of open window sleeping. But spring is the most wonderful season.

Privileged as I feel to lie here and absorb all this music, all the beauty and energy that surrounds this bed and our open window, I can't bring myself to lie here for another minute.

There are far too many things happening on the other side of the window that I want to be a part of. I want to welcome every returning bird, every unfolding flower, emerging butterfly, and sprouting seed. I want to find every hidden fawn lying in the tall grass, every bird nest in the branches of trees or on the ground. I want to know where the raccoons sleep during the day and where the sharp-shinned hawk sleeps at night. I want to know where the barred owls have their nest. I want to lift up rocks and turn over rotting logs so I can find every impossibly colored salamander that lives here. I want to find the black snakes in the forest canopy and the box turtles plodding along under flaming azaleas. I want to sit by the stream and listen to her song, watch the dragonflies dart here and there, backwards and forwards. I want to find the old woodpeckers' hole in the sycamore tree that overhangs the water's edge and see if the wood ducks are nesting there again this spring. I want to sit still and silent in the tall grass at the edge of the bank and watch the great blue heron spear a fish. I want to climb to a ridgetop, watch the mountainside turn green with new life, and be carried down into the valleys on a vibrant swath of emerald.

I would like to float in the air with a turkey vulture, then dance with a west wind. To squeeze every ounce of energy, wisdom, and grace from this season. This season that passes so quickly. This is my desire, my quest. If it were up to me, I would never leave the forest until June. Then having been totally saturated in "wildness," completely filled with witnessing countless miracles and confident that I could keep all her mysteries a secret, I would emerge, my clothes and beard smelling like a garden after a storm, wet leaves, wildflowers, and pine needles.

There are ghosts who live here. They travel in herds of four or six; often there are many more. They are gentle and quiet. You can look right at them and not see them, unless they move.

Sometimes, when I drive down our road it frightens them and they leap into the woods, white tails flashing. Then they disappear. They seem to dematerialize before your eyes. One day, my wife was coming home, and a herd was in the woods just off the road. She would have missed the gathering, but a shaft of sunlight had found its way through the forest and illuminated the sides of their faces. The beauty of that moment took her breath away.

I want so many things this time of year. But mostly I want to remain aware, and I want to remain grateful. I don't know how many spring seasons are left to me. I don't know what a spring would be like if age took away even one of my five senses. But this morning, through an open window, I will experience them all.

Spring in the Blue Ridge Mountains (Brown Thrashers, Black Snakes, and Chickadees)

The brown thrasher picked up a small stick, she turned it this way and that, dropped it on the ground and picked it up again. I watched her test it over and over, running her beak back and forth from one end to the other, pressing the tip against the ground judging its pliability. Finally, she discarded it altogether and picked another. It too, was subjected to the same rigorous standards used to gauge its usefulness. Her examination was precise; instinctively she knew what was required, and so intent was she on this important task, she seemed unaware I was only several yards from where she was working. When she finally settled on which stick would best suit her purposes, she flew into a small thicket and strategically placed the chosen twig amongst some others. She poked and pushed and pulled as the twig was woven into the small shallow bowl; it was just the framework, the beginning of her nest.

Only about four feet off the ground, it appeared vulnerable to predators and I found it odd that she continued to work while I stood so close. No attempt was made to conceal the nest site, drive me away, or distract me. She may have been a first-year mother with little experience so I thought it best to leave her to the work at hand

31

and check on her progress the next day. Similar in size to the robin with a longer tail that often angles upward like a wren, they have a bright rufous color on their upper parts and a buff-white on their lower parts with prominent black streaking and two white wing bars. They can be rather stern looking with a slightly curved bill and intense yellow eyes.

The brown thrasher is a prolific and accomplished vocalist and may sing over eleven hundred different song types including imitations of other birds. They are a favorite bird of my wife, not just because of their beauty and musical repertoire, but their bold personalities make them fun to watch. A rare presence around our property, because we live deep in the woods.

They prefer spaces that border a woodlot and fields that have been abandoned where thick bushes like hawthorns grow. Much of their time is spent skulking in the undergrowth, rummaging under leaf litter and grasses, swishing their beaks back and forth, throwing debris off to the sides in search of insects—mainly beetles—and other arthropods, seeds, and fruit.

Between 1966 and 2015, populations of brown thrashers have declined by 41% according to the "North American Breeding Bird Survey." Like all birds they suffer from habitat loss, and die from exposure to pesticides as well as natural predators like sharp-shinned hawks.

In the United States alone, it is estimated that the domestic house cat kills from 1.4 billion to 3.7 billion birds a year. Cell towers and skyscrapers kill millions more as birds that migrate often fly at night and whole flocks are killed when they collide with these structures that are unnaturally tall; and, of course, cars kill many millions more. With statistics like these, one has to wonder how there are any birds left at all.

At almost sixty years old, I hear how quiet the forests and meadows have become since I was a boy. It happens so slowly, over many decades; few hardly notice.

When I arrived back home, my wife and daughter were defending a chickadees' nest that had been built in a birdhouse positioned high off the ground on our back deck. A four-foot black snake had found his way up the stairs and was scoping out any meal opportunities that were present.

Black snakes are fantastic climbers and, in our area, spend most of their time in the forest canopy where bird and squirrel nests are easy pickings. Last summer I watched as a six-foot black snake devoured a nest full of half-grown blue jays. The parents as well as other adult jays came streaking in from all directions to help defend the nest, but it was no use. Two of the fledglings managed to escape by jumping from the nest that was almost forty feet up in a pine tree. The other three were swallowed whole as the jay community watched in horror. Their dive bombing, screams, and well-placed pecking did little to slow the inevitable.

I pushed this new opportunist off the deck with my foot and it landed with a thud on the soft forest floor. The chickadees' nest survived another day. Like house cats, black snakes are great for helping to keep the rodent population under control. Unfortunately, like house cats, they also kill birds and can't distinguish between a rare breed and ones that are plentiful.

They are both indiscriminate killers. While the snake may only kill and eat once or twice a month, a cat is a constant hunter and kills whenever it can, regardless of hunger. In fact, a well-fed cat is a more efficient hunter.

Black snakes are oviparous, meaning they lay eggs. The "gravid" female will lay between six and thirty smooth leathery eggs in mid to late July. Females only reproduce about every three years in the colder parts of their range, but possibly every year in the warmer regions. The eggs are laid under logs or in hollow trees and the young (about twelve inches at hatching) typically stay in the area of the nest for the first couple of years, even hibernating together at the nest site. The snakes are prey as well and have many predators, starting with the burying beetle which lays its eggs in the snake's eggs and the beetle larvae parasitize the developing embryos by feeding on them.

Over next few days I checked on the thrasher's progress. The nest was only a little more developed; it was as though she had lost interest. After a week it was obvious—she had abandoned the site or was killed by a predator. I never saw her again after that first day and I never saw a mate. Perhaps her mate was killed and that's why the nest was abandoned.

Even an astute observer can only speculate on the many passionate struggles that unfold in nature just beyond the windows of our comfortable, safe homes. I became anxious about the chickadees' nest and pulled open the front of the nest box. A beautiful, articulately crafted nest crowded the interior. It was made from moss, lichen, and small delicate grasses. I spread apart an unbelievably soft layer of feather down covering six tiny white and brown mottled eggs and gently ran my fingers across their surface; they felt like warm, but delicate jellybeans. Knowing there was a life force growing inside each one suddenly gave me pause and I knew I had taken my curiosity too far. Six tiny magic jewels, enchanting and mysterious. Only the incubators understood their true value. I withdrew my hand and closed the box.

I knew a man once who called chickadees: "Elves of the forest." I think that's an accurate description. They are bold and sassy little birds that tame easily and will feed from your hand. I had taken no more than three steps from the nest box and a parent dove from a tree branch, scolded me for my transgression, and entered the box in a huff without even a sideways glance.

It's late May and the forest is thriving and full of activity. It seems as though there is movement everywhere you look. What you can't see can often be heard. The chorus starts before first light—wrens, cardinals, wood thrush, eastern phoebe and wood peewees, jays, ravens, warblers, and others, calling out territory. Though some mornings as we lie in bed with windows open it seems they are singing for pure joy and greet the new day with an enthusiasm that comes from knowing their Creator personally. Box turtles, salamanders painted with fantastic colors, newts, and insects that defy identification prowl the forest floor. Weasels, mink, raccoons, opossums, deer, fox, squirrels, rabbits, and bear play their roles without complaint, and butterflies, humming birds, bees, and other pollinators work tirelessly.

The resident pair of barred owls call back and forth across the ravine at dusk. All through the night, one very lonely spring peeper calls and calls waiting for a reply. He may have hitched a ride in one of our kayaks while we were out exploring the river and found himself trapped here in the woods. There are no others.

By mid-June things will have calmed down somewhat. The forest breathes a soothing sigh of relief; the pulse that summer brings feels slower. Parent birds are quiet when the young have left the nest. There is no reason to draw attention to their position. I'll tend our garden and delight in the cool earth on my bare feet, and feel the weight of a thousand eyes; aware that the activity that surrounds us is beyond comprehension. Under the soil, in the trees, in the air, there is life, vibrant, mysterious, passionate. You can taste it, but you don't know what you're tasting; you feel it, but don't understand why the hairs on your neck rise. You hear whispers, and shadows slip by the corners of your eye. It is the spirit of the forest and all of its inhabitants from the beginning of time. The spirit of God never resting, still creating, still courting, and in love with creation.

Midsummer Mornings

This morning, the trees of the forest are dark and dripping with moisture. Bizarre looking mushrooms and colorful fungi have risen from brown pine needles, decaying leaves, and fallen trees. Invisible forces are at work turning them into humus for future generations. Spider webs crafted in the night now hang low, bejeweled with dew. And somewhere beyond the forest, a misty, glowing light is trying to penetrate this natural amphitheater.

There are creatures that have occasion to pass through here. Their passion plays, dramatic life and death struggles, even their comedies, can turn the grounds into a vaudeville stage. On this moody, gray morning it's an opera house for the grandstanding aria of the pileated woodpecker and the competing whimsical song of a wood thrush.

For me, it's a lecture hall and I am compelled to listen. So quiet is the voice for such an ardent narrative. Some days, I come away not understanding the lesson, but am always left with a quiet peace. It's as though I've been in the presence of infinite grace, welcoming acceptance and inspiration. I've come to realize that it's a place I go to heal.

Lately, I feel the burden of trust left to me by an old man that may have expected something more from the time we spent together. I should be doing more for these wild places.

Intimate Strangers

My wife and I share our space with an interesting cast of characters. There are Gus and Gertie: two German Shepherds who seem to accept us as adequate care givers. Gus who has had more than his fair share of tragic accidents and near fatal diseases has an adoring, but ever so needy sidekick in Gertie, who never wanders very far from his side.

The pair can be found most days, waiting patiently on the front porch for a human escort to accompany them on one of their many strolls about the grounds. And an escort is necessary most days, because there is a stealthy band of thugs that patrol the area waiting for an opportunity to lay waste to unsuspecting innocents. Webbed feet slapping down hard in quick succession and a short hiss is all one is likely to hear before being accosted with a shocking nip to the inner thigh or calf muscle. My wife has a stick that she takes with her whenever she steps outside. "Run fast screaming, and carry a big stick" is her motto. I think it's funny . . . she, is not amused. But then they don't bother me. I guess they bonded with me as goslings. I'm like their gang leader. They follow me around chatting me up and if I sit down, they come up to me and tell me stories while they untie my shoelaces.

Clarence, the big white goose with the large carbuncle like knot on his forehead, likes to be picked up and placed in my lap where he can feel superior. Thaddeus, the other male, doesn't seem to mind. But he is getting older and lately he has this look in his eye, like he may be channeling Charles Manson or Al Capone. Either way, I get the feeling he's making plans of a nefarious nature for my untimely demise.

Of course, I have a noisy entourage that follows up the driveway when I feed the chickens. You never can tell; an unsuspecting hen may need to be reminded who the bosses are around here. The large rooster gets the respect his size commands. He's the last one. His two friends got aggressive with my wife and found themselves mixed with wild rice and vegetables. Some hens are missing as well. Victims of our resident Cooper's and red-tailed hawks.

We've had other animals that stayed for a short time. Crows, hawks, owls, and baby raccoons all needing a little rehab. Some extra help to be on their way. But it's the locals that we have come to appreciate. Flying squirrels that come at night to the feeder by the dozen. Gliding on invisible zip lines they come in from all directions. Frantic lunatics in need of a Ritalin prescription. They're chaotic gathering on our back porch is more entertaining than anything on

TV. Sometimes they let you get close enough to touch them—their fur as soft as eider down.

There is a black snake here as well; he lived in a cement block on our basement wall that has a small chunk missing. One day I came out the basement door with a dead mouse that I removed from a trap. He was sunning himself on the lawn. I walked up to him very slowly and offered him the mouse. His tongue flicked out, tasting the air for microscopic particles that identified what was being offered. Rather than strike quickly and coil around his prey which would have been the normal reaction, he slowly and gently took the mouse from my hand and swallowed it head first. I walked away under the gaze of cold, unblinking eyes. I still see him occasionally; he's grown considerably since then. Too big to fit back in his cement block. I wonder where he stays now?

Some years ago, my brother-in-law gave me a box turtle that he had kept in an aquarium. He named him Houdini because he was always escaping from his quarters. Obviously, Houdini felt he needed to be somewhere else and wasn't happy, so my brother-in-law asked if I would take him and perhaps release him on our property. I did. I see Houdini now and again every summer. I know it's him because he has a chip missing from the back of his carapace. He shows up in our front yard or on the driveway. I've offered him sweet juicy strawberries and other turtle delicacies, but he has always refused.

Pileated woodpeckers are striking! They are the largest woodpecker in North America and about the size of a crow. Jet black with bright white stripes across their face and down their necks and a flaming red crest. A dashing, arrogant bird that pounds large rectangular holes in trees, tearing out chunks of wood the size of your thumb while searching out colonies of carpenter ants, wood beetles, and insect larvae of all kinds. Their old nesting holes are used by small owls, wood ducks, bats, pine martins and I'm sure, flying squirrels. The pileated call is loud and primeval. Like something out of the Amazon rain forest. We have a resident pair. I am made aware of their presence almost every day. If I don't see them when out walking, I hear them calling back and forth to each other or hacking away on a tree somewhere deep in the woods like a man with an ax.

Last summer I was lying out in a reclining lawn chair in the front yard when a fearless and handsome avian acrobat came swooping down from the trees and landed on a rooted stump I had put in the garden not five feet from where I was sitting. He ignored me as he went about searching for a possible meal hiding inside the stump. He was strong and sure of himself, a real professional. His eyes were bright and focused on the job at hand. A prehistoric looking creature so full of himself, I couldn't help but admire him. We had a friend who lived close by who loved these birds. She would get so excited whenever she saw them. She died suddenly last fall. Whenever I see them now, I think of her.

We live in paradise and have become intimate with the holiness that surrounds us. The government lets me believe I own some property here so they can extract taxes for the privilege of that fantasy. But I know the truth. I'm merely a temporary caretaker of something perfect. If the powers that be decide they want to run an oil pipeline through here, or a power line right of way, or if they find something of value underground, they will cancel my privilege and take what they want. I have faith that will never happen.

We do have intimacy here with the others who share our space. Strangers once. But no more. And what are we to them? Sometimes I wonder. Last fall I was sitting in a chair on the back porch and a nuthatch landed on my leg. It seemed to have no fear, so I reached out and stroked its head with my finger. After a few seconds it flew up on the railing a few feet away. How did he know not to be afraid, that I wouldn't hurt him? Maybe he's been watching me . . . and decided it was time to have intimacy with a stranger.

Autumn

It's been several weeks since the last hummingbird darted from the feeder. Across the garden, yellow maple leaves float in place of swallowtail butterflies, then stick to wet, flat stones on the garden path. It rained hard last night. Morning's first light filtered through a lead gray sky, and was welcomed by a lone wren singing solo. Last night, I listened to a single cricket give what sounded like his final serenade. There will be warmer sunny days, before winter closes her hand on autumn's time. But for now, a bumble bee's dance on hyssop is over, the butterfly battles have ceased, and dragonfly patrols just above garden blooms have ended.

The hillsides have offered up this season's palette of fall colors and paint the earth with yellows, reds, and rust. Trees of the forest feel like a gathering of friends—one last celebration before deep slumber. The trail this morning is hushed, as though everything is listening intently. Leaves are softened from the rain and my footsteps are quiet. I am not so careful where I walk today, a much more destructive force has preceded me, and there is nothing left for a boot print to harm.

The long migration has ended for another season and birds that remain seem to be living in a neighborhood abandoned. But no, they are the gatekeepers. Spring brings with her avian refugees, pilgrims, immigrants, and opportunists of all sorts. Not as many as years before, but still they come, driven by the desire to survive and perpetuate their kind in a diminished land. They have not come to merely escape from something, but into something. As Joseph Wood Crutch wrote: "They are part of the greatest community, not of man alone, but of everything that shares with us the great adventure of being alive!"

So autumn is here, and she prepares the earth for rest. At times, I too, can hear her voice, feel her comforting wisdom, and know a peace in the realization of how much will remain undone when the season ends.

September

Summer's end comes steadily with a low angled sun. Morning shadows reveal flimsy spider webs that hang low, bejeweled with dew. The sun rises later and sets a little earlier. There is increased activity as everything senses time is running short. Humming birds hit the feeder in greater numbers as their migration south across the gulf has already begun.

Buck with velvety antlers stalk the forest as ginger ghosts, leaving signs of their passing with gouged out areas of earth and rubbed off bark hanging in strips from the trunks of saplings. Turkeys roam the woods in small flocks like gossiping church ladies in petticoats. And bears, black silhouettes, plodding amid an emerald world digging up, pulling down or turning over anything that might reveal precious calories to support a long winter.

Every creature that lives here can feel it. A gentle prodding, reminding us change is coming. With that knowledge comes a peace, sometimes tinged with melancholy. Another summer is ending. And how many more are left to us?

But today, the sky could not be a cleaner blue. The sun tries to deceive us with her embrace and the air is yet to be filled with the scent of rotting leaves. So, we revel in the knowledge that September is here and everyday forward is a gift. Soon the snow will cover a sleeping land, and spring will come again.

First Snow

There is something about falling snow that brings a peace. Not wind-swept blizzards with accompanying whiteouts and five-foot drifts that keep one snowbound and restless for days.

But a gentle snow, that falls quietly to brush against the dried beech and oak leaves that continue to cling to their branches. It piles up gradually with a quiet determination that seems effortless, and accumulates in the boughs of the pines until weight lowers the branch and releases its crystals in a cascading white shower sometimes bathed in the prism of reflective light. Its ability to transform a landscape by morning's light leaves a person wondering if they had somehow been transported to another world as they slept.

Even in the city, a snowfall leaves a neighborhood in a quiet calm, the urban sprawl layered in an insulating cover of white, a pause in the comings and goings of so many; just as it does in the forest or meadow spaces. All living things seem to falter for just a moment to re-adjust their lives and perspective.

From our window it's a dreamscape waiting for exploration. Cedar rails attached to fence posts punctuated with a generous mantle of white, bushes spread apart from the weight, everything familiar, now laminated with a purity untouched.

"Farmer's Almanac says this winter will be wet and mild," my wife reminds me as she laces up her boots. The dogs do a happy dance on the front porch in anticipation of joining the people they adore in one of their favorite activities. They jump and pounce in the snow. Even Gus our older dog, who on some days has trouble walking, finds new energy and brings his head up from the snow with a four-inch nose cone and tries to entice us all into a game we know he can no longer play. Our boots squeak and crunch in the snow and are accompanied by the sound of heavy, happy panting. They keep looking behind to make sure we're still coming and haven't veered off to start some chore or project. They want to believe this is their time now; family time. As important to them as it was to us when we still had our children at home.

I like to look for fresh tracks left in the snow by our wild neighbors. I'd follow them if the dogs weren't with us. They would only plow through the snow, destroying clues to the story. It occurs to me while I write this essay, that the tiny black shapes I leave on a white page create a picture and tell a story in the minds of those who can interpret their meaning. For me it's the same, following the telltale paw prints, broken branches, chunks of fur, a scattering of feathers, or drops of scarlet left behind on the white surface. A narrative begins to emerge outlining the most intimate accounts of survival and adventure, as engaging as any well written novel.

Back home now, warm and secure, a melancholy seems to flow over me. Is it the quiet calm of the forest landscape under a cold gray sky, or the winter season almost upon us? And with it, do you not sometimes feel an absence of hope? Days like these can be a time for introspection.

A lifetime gone by already, with our own share of tragedy, grief and loss, but also, adventure, joy and uncompromising love. If I were ever to lose my wife, who would be left that could ever understand; as hers are the same? As usual, we are connected. The tears that run down her face this afternoon do not require an explanation. So, we'll sit, and hold each other's hands, and wait for love and gratitude to overpower despair. And in so doing, follow nature's lead, for in all her acts she reflects nothing but her faith in the future.

She has written her endorsement of Emerson's words: "The sun will shine after every storm; there is a solution for every problem; and the soul's highest duty is to be of good cheer."

My wife reminds me again, "The Farmer's Almanac says that this winter will be wet and mild."

Life's Seasons

The moon is almost full. Its light soft. Her shadows long and silent. At three o'clock in the morning, I am unsettled on the front porch repeating a mantra of peace in the quiet transition of night and day.

Change is coming. As unstoppable as the seasons, recognized and understood in small but subtle differences each day, each week. It's high summer, but this morning autumn whispered her intent. Her breath warms the side of my face.

I embrace change, require change, am stimulated by change. But I've never been this age. Autumn comes for both of us it seems. Summer has no fear, she'll be back when the sun is angled high and the days are long.

My life's summer season is slipping from my hand, her finger tips brushing across my palm, waiting for my grateful acknowledgment of her gifts. The departure is making me feel vulnerable. I can almost see her walking away turning one last time to say goodbye, leaving me with autumn. I don't know her well. But she doesn't seem as though she'll be as compatible for the journey.

Often on nights like these, when the forest is so illuminated, I've wanted to wander, to feel her mysteries in a different light. But I am not a nocturnal being, and the woods at night is unfamiliar and may do me harm. There are bears, poisonous snakes, and spiders. I would be at a disadvantage, vulnerable.

Suddenly, I was outraged that I felt vulnerable. I went in the house and picked up the blue flashlight. It's made from steel, is long and heavy from the weight of four large batteries. But I didn't need it, the moon provided light enough. What I wanted was something that could be used as a weapon. The realization made me even more angry. I left the flashlight on the porch and walked up our long winding driveway, alone. The dogs whined and pawed at the gate, confused.

When I came to the gravel road I hesitated. This seemed like it was far enough. Fear has a way of making your senses come alive. I stood in the middle of the road, closed my eyes, and tried to see with my ears. The sound of snapping branches close by covered me with goose bumps but I refused to open my eyes. I just listened . . . and waited.

With age comes humility. Acknowledgment of being powerless to stop time. Age also gives power—power of wisdom and hindsight. Power that comes from recovering from great loss and sorrow. Power that comes from learning how to love and allowing yourself to be loved. Power that comes from liking who you have become. And power that comes in finding truth, and the freedom to let go of religion and superstition.

Across the road from our driveway is a trail that escorts one to the top of a ridge line. A pathway, little more than a high tunnel meandering through a swath of emerald, and illuminated now by the calming moonlight. It leads to the vertex with an inspiring vista. But trees have grown too tall, too thick, and in summer provide an obstruction to the panorama.

An increasing trepidation was forcing its way past my resolve to be invincible, or at least, less vulnerable. I opened my eyes and looked into the trail. God, but it was beautiful. I've passed it countless times at night as I come home, but my headlights hide the beauty of nature's luminescence.

I was startled by movement in a branch overhead. A great horned owl! Was he here the whole time, or did he fly in when my eyes were closed? An owl's flight is silent, their feathers covered in small hooks and bows that break up air turbulence. Any remaining noise is reduced by velvety downy feathers on their wings and legs. Those soft feathers absorb high frequency sounds other animals are sensitive to. A perfect design. The moon was so bright I could see the yellow in his big round eyes. He seemed to have a curious regard for my presence. Lifting one foot from his perch, placing it back down. Then the other. All the while bobbing his head in a circular motion as if trying to focus on what he was looking at. It would seem I had been given a guardian. His presence certainly distracted me from my nervousness. I wasn't alone, but then one never is while in the forest. Perhaps, I will walk that trail after all.

All my senses on high alert, I stepped off the road and onto the mossy ground. I was tempted to remove my sandals, but I know what this trail looks like in the daylight. Rocks, fallen branches, and pine cones litter the ground, several holes where skunks have dug out yellow jacket nests lie in wait to twist an ankle and always, the possibility of copperheads.

Katydids, by the thousands, fill the air with their summertime chorus. A screech owl somewhere far off, wails a tender, lonesome cry. Different voices drift through the forest at night. Whip-poor-will, once common in the area, are rare to hear now, as are barred owls. Coyotes would come howling and yipping as they ran through the hollows and across the ridge lines, but a bounty has been placed on their heads, so their songs have gone quiet as well. I looked behind me to see if the owl was still there. He was not.

It wasn't possible to walk quietly. Too many small twigs and crunchy pine cones. I've never minded getting older. Never thought about it much. When I turned thirty, I felt empowered, the same at forty. I had really hit my stride at fifty and always enjoyed good health and athletic strength. But never have I felt the rushing of time so apparent or so poignant as I have these last few weeks.

The end of the trail opens up to a small clearing and a star-filled sky. A westerly wind blew down across the ridge and pushed up against my body. I had a keen desire to remove all my clothes and dance with her a while in a lovers' embrace across the rolling hills, and down into hidden valleys. What secrets unfold there in the early hours of dawn? I would tell no one.

Standing here, looking up at the moon, I realized there are many things I know, many things I've learned, that can't be translated into words. So, I can't pass them on. Not even to my own children. My understanding of the natural world is where my true intimacy lies and it's what I would love to teach. It's how I could change the world. Time is short and I have yet to learn how to translate that gift.

Technology has become the enemy of reverence. We have become so dazzled by our own inventions and in the process, creation seems so much less. Maybe a few will be drawn to her by people like me, by our strong faith and the beauty of our personal lives that comes from that intimacy.

The sun will be trading places soon. I should go back. My dogs and my wife will worry.

Life is long. Life is hard. And life is oh so beautiful. Something happens every day that takes my breath away. Something happens every day that breaks my heart. Even if it's the memory of someone we loved, no longer here. It's as much a privilege to feel sorrow as it is to feel joy. Life is long. Time is short.

High Drama in Tall Trees

I wondered what all the commotion was about. Blue jays streaking through the air screaming out alarms at the top of their lungs. Sounds of panic and turmoil. I looked around and saw two fledglings on the ground. Still too young to fly, maybe a week or so from leaving the nest voluntarily. I picked them up and put them in what I thought would be a safe place where the parents still had access to them. The parents were distraught, calling out to them and dive bombing me. I withdrew to a safe vantage point where I could watch and not cause any more stress to the family than necessary.

They didn't stay put long. Robins, who must have had a nest nearby, attacked the young jays, which brought down the wrath of the already adrenaline-charged parents. A terrible fight erupted with more screams and feathers flying. The rumble tumbled into the territory of a pair of tufted titmice who also joined in on the melee. This time of year is nesting season, birds take up residence and have rigid boundaries that are strictly enforced.

Territories may overlap, but it's usually a matter of height not depth that are of concern. Blue jays like the high canopy, robins and other thrushes prefer the lower ground cover, and chickadees and the titmice take up residence in the middle area. I walk this section of woods every day and consider myself an astute observer of my surroundings and the creatures I share our space with. But I'd never noticed these nests before or was even remotely aware of the family life going on around me. I decided it would be best if I left and let nature sort itself out.

When I reached the house, my wife asked what all the commotion was about. She could hear the ruckus from the front porch. When I explained, she questioned my logic in leaving the defenseless young on the ground and wondered about their ability to survive a night on the forest floor. She isn't one who would normally advocate for intervention, but there was something about the continued screams from the blue jay parents that begged further inspection.

Other jays now were streaking in from different directions all calling alarms. The nest was not hard to find, several of the birds were panicked and jumped from branch to branch and dove at the clump of sticks and forest litter that made up the nest. It was about forty feet up, and nestled in a branch close to the trunk of a white pine. Now I could see what the real problem was. A huge black snake was coiled around the branches and nest gulping down the remaining nestlings while the parents and neighboring jays tried valiantly to drive back the enemy. They screamed and dove and pecked, risking their own lives in the process. But it was all for naught.

The parents flew back and forth from the nest to an area in the woods where I assumed the young that had made their escape had settled.

Night was coming. I thought about snakes and screech owls, raccoons and weasels, opportunists who work the night shift. The jay remaining young would not make it till the morning light. We looked and looked but couldn't find the nestlings. Well, I thought, maybe they'll be safe. But I knew otherwise. We walked back to the house followed by the aria of what sounded to me, like weeping parents. Rarely do we have to think about the suffering of the creatures of our forests, their life's dramas and passion plays, carried out just beyond the safety of our windows. Who thinks about a mother witnessing her babies being swallowed alive by a snake?

They don't feel love or loss the way we do. It's only a bird. Not a being like us. Therefore, they must be less. The actions of these parents and their defending neighbors would suggest otherwise.

It's true that blue jays are responsible for their own share of grief to other birds when they steal eggs or hatchlings from nests. But there is no malice involved, no evil intent. Just like the black snake, it's a matter of survival. I went back and kept searching.

Finally, first one, then the other. They are in a box in my living room now. And I am out in the yard looking for bugs that will make a tasty meal until I can buy the ingredients that will make up their new diet. One that can be squeezed through a syringe for convenience.

The forest is quiet now. However I can't help but believe, that somewhere close, is great mourning in the heart of a mother, who today, in a matter of minutes, lost her family.

Four-week-old blue jay.

The Woodlands of Ivor

Ten-week-old blue jay.

Sharon's Geese

When I was fourteen, I bought a baby goose, a gosling, only a day or two old. I put him with four young chicks and three young ducklings. They all grew up together. None of them seemingly knew what they were or that they were different from one another. I had to make a dramatic rescue one day when the chickens followed the goose and ducks into the stream in our back yard. Apparently, none of them knew they couldn't swim. They floated helplessly on their sides towards a four-foot waterfall. Pretty funny really. To be fair, chickens aren't the brightest of fowl.

The goose, "Waldo," was no trouble. He fell in love with Daisy the white duck and got a little aggressive when he thought she was being threatened in any way. Our pet crow "Inky" picked up on this right away and made Waldo's life a living hell. Constant harassment was his objective and he was successful. But Waldo and his little harem were fun to watch and care for.

So now, some forty years later, I think about dear Waldo and wonder about acquiring another goose. I don't have a stream, pond, or any water to speak of on my property but still somehow think having a goose would be nice. My ever so selfless and compassionate wife never thought to question my reasoning or qualifications for goose ownership, but only wanted for me the desires of my heart. So, my search began. We live in farm country but no one seemed to have any geese. *Hmmm.* That should have been my first clue. An online search brought up a hatchery in another state, but they would ship no less than eight hatchlings per order. Well, that could only mean eight times the fun, right? I was undaunted. I put in my information, hit the order button and waited for a call from the post office. In the meantime, I made a place ready for them. Food . . . check, water . . . check, heat lamp . . . check, safe place out of harm's way . . . check. When the call came, one day later than expected. I rushed down to pick up the magic box that contained the new life that would share our home. Sadly, when I opened the box, four were DOA. That extra day without food or water was too much for the weaker ones.

They must have shipped them within minutes of hatching as the egg shells were still in the box.

Four soft, fluffy, yellow goslings peeped all the way home. I had no idea what kind they were.

It was a mixed batch. They could be any one of five different breeds. That was the deal when I ordered them. Of course, my wife fell in love instantly. Who wouldn't? Perhaps someone who knew what was waiting in the not-so-distant future. She held them in her hands and brought them up to her face and lovingly told each one how beautiful and precious it was.

She sat with them out in the back yard and they all gathered around Mother Sharon's feet peeping and pulling up grassy snacks. When she got up to move, they dutifully followed her wherever she went. They were of course, adorable. A little gaggle of cuteness. Always together, always peeping and always finding trouble. Like the Keystone Cops with webbed feet.

The dogs were only mildly amused. Sharing their already limited attention with yet another added group to a steadily growing menagerie was troublesome. They were taking a wait and see approach.

Spring turned to summer and summer to fall. They grew rapidly and it wasn't long before we could identify the breeds. A pair of Chinese White and a pair of Pomeranians. They outgrew one cage, then another. Finally, they were allowed free range of the place during the day but placed in safe quarters for the night. Our home is in the woods and many would-be predators work the night shift.

Sharon bought them a small "kiddie pool" from Walmart to swim in. We'd fill it and pull up a couple of chairs and watch them play, swim, and bathe. They were pretty comical. They liked everyone and got along just fine with the dogs, chickens, and visiting human family and friends.

As they got a little bigger, my wife, who for some reason has always been nervous around birds, began to shy away from their advances. This was around the same time they were reaching adolescence and started to adopt a surly attitude about their personal space. They picked up on Sharon's nervousness immediately and took full advantage of the opportunity to be dominant and have the upper hand. At first, they would lull her into a false sense of security by pretending to be all social and needy. When they had her surrounded, they would close ranks and nip at her legs and shoes. I would hear her pitiful cries for help mixed with their incessant high-pitched, glee-filled honking and come running to the rescue. Sometimes she was frozen with fear, too afraid to move. The geese took this for open season on the gullible and intensified their attack. To my wife's credit, she was not calling for their heads as she did for the roosters who showed her the same contempt and threw themselves on her at will.

Sharon took to arming herself when she had to leave the house and walk to the car or do any chores around the perimeter of her safe zone. A stick, a shovel, or rake. One day I saw her with a pitch fork cautiously looking both ways before opening the gate and stepping out into the "combat zone." Years ago, she spent one full summer a virtual prisoner in her own house because of a pet raven who had decided it didn't like the competition Sharon represented for my attention. After that, she was determined to become a stoic warrior in defense of her right to lead a full and rewarding life on the outside. I applauded her resolve, but it melted away every time some bird sensed her apprehension and turned aggressive.

I received a call one day. Sharon was sobbing from her prison inside our truck. She had gone to feed the chickens and the last rooster that had not yet made it to the chopping block, chased her all the way to the vehicle jabbing her with his spurs the whole distance. This was no joke! He was a huge bird. Easily fifteen pounds. Because my sense of humor is perverse, I laughed. As it turns out, this was not the appropriate thing for me to do. Redemption came only when I followed through with my promise that the bird would not witness another sunrise. We had chicken for dinner that evening. Sharon however, despite her injuries is not a vengeful person and did not enjoy the meal. She truly wants to befriend these animals and resents the fear she has that seems to promote some of the aggression towards her. I don't know how to help her.

The geese continued to make her life difficult. They also started to go after visiting friends and the dogs. Everyone but me. I would go outside and they would follow me around telling me their stories and if I sat down in a chair or on the grass they would gather around, untie my shoelaces and gently pull on my clothes.

I came home one day and when I walked through the door Sharon's finger was in my face.

"Look," she said. "Something needs to be done about those geese!"

Sharon's best friend in the world is Terry. Terry loves animals and just has this "need" to touch everything.

We were camping once in Okefenokee swamp down in Georgia and there was a ten-foot alligator soaking up some rays at the side of the road. He was minding his own business not hurting a soul. Terry had to touch him. She walked up to it and stroked its tail. She's one of those people you read about that end up hospitalized after being gored by a buffalo in Yellowstone.

Terry was determined to make friends with the geese and had made great progress. They love apples. So, she took some apples out and began feeding them, talking to them real sweet like. All was going well until without warning they decided she had stepped over some invisible line. They pinned her up against the car and were taking turns pinching hunks of flesh and slapping her with their wings. Sharon heard the screams for help and ran outside to rescue her friend. I could only imagine the chaotic scene. This time I didn't laugh, not out loud anyway. I promised I would find them a new home.

Everyone I asked that I thought was a good candidate for goose ownership gave me a one-word answer. "No!" Mr. Cox who has a farm and lots of space had a two-word answer: "Hell no!"

We fenced in a large area close to the house so I could hear if anyone bothered them at night and I built a small building for them to get out of the cold in the winter and we locked them up. In the minds of the geese our actions were indefensible. The decibel level of their vocal pleas and protests every time we stepped out the door or worked in the yard made it impossible to carry on any kind of meaningful conversation. In the end it was Sharon who confessed, "I feel sorry for them." (Insert here your own vision of the probable look on my face.) The geese made parole and Sharon started spending more time in the house.

They made it past their first winter and by spring they started laying eggs. Big beautiful delicious eggs. I was hoping they would have a more "gamey" taste but were virtually indistinguishable from what our chickens were offering. However, they were three times the cholesterol and fat. We gave some away to people who made painted Easter eggs and Sharon hollowed out others to paint and make decorations for our Christmas tree.

The eggs were a nice added treat but being protective over a couple of nests made them even more aggressive. They even took a couple of swipes my way. Anything they thought represented a danger was subject to attack. Even if I was carrying something that looked suspicious, like a bucket of feed or water.

Getting out of the car with grocery bags in hand turned out to be an incredible violation worthy of the most severe punishment. Any time company pulled up I would have to go outside and provide a safe escort to the house. If we knew ahead of time someone was coming over, we'd check and see where they were. If they were in the back yard, we were good. If they were out front an attack was imminent. So, I would go outside and herd them into their pen for the safety of our guests, and to assure our continued friendship.

Their aggression had certainly become a major problem but there were other issues. There was no place that was off-limits to them. Few things in life can be more annoying than a foursome of bossy geese who just don't understand that not everything belongs to them. The vegetable gardens and flower gardens had to be fenced, and the sheer number of "goose poop land mines" was staggering, so the walkways had to be fenced and gated as well. The place was starting to look like an internment camp.

When things happen slowly over a long period of time you don't notice the inconvenience as much. When they weren't attacking the chickens, dogs, or humans and when they weren't pooping everywhere or getting into the gardens, they were kind of fun to have around. Like four miniature dinosaurs roaming the grounds. Sometimes I would look out the window and their bodies would be concealed behind a long row of bushes or plants and just their heads would be visible, floating along in single file on patrol and alert to everything—nothing escaped inspection.

On occasion, when they're in the mood, they'll accompany us on our walks with the dogs. Up our long winding driveway, across the road, down a path through the forest and home again.

The little gaggle following behind in single file chatting the whole way, their bodies rocking back and forth on stubby little legs but their heads always straight and level. They somehow make you feel as though it's a privilege having them along.

"Thaddeus" the large Pomeranian male is always on guard and will let out a scream at a decibel level that is truly impressive whenever danger lurks close by. "Clarence" the male Chinese White always has to have the last word and sticks his tongue out whenever he verbalizes so it sounds like he's talking with a lisp. "Iris" the female Chinese White is just a bitch and doesn't like anyone. She has a voice that sounds like a duck and "quacks" more than honks. "Monica" is the female Pomeranian and our favorite. She has this lovely voice that sounds like cascading laughter. She is the most curious of the lot, always lagging behind, never in a hurry. She's gentle and has a subtle calm that radiates from her eyes. But when you walk outside and they all come up to greet you they sound like a bunch of squeaky gates in need of oiling.

I believe in being responsible for the animals we acquire. It was my choice to have these geese. It's not their fault I'm an idiot and didn't think a little longer and harder about having them as residents here. So, I don't think it's right to punish them for being . . . well, geese. But my wife lives here as well and I promised her I would try to find them another home. For me, that means a better home. After exhausting all possibilities here, I remembered a couple I did a job for several years ago, in North Carolina. They had a beautiful spread.

Over thirty acres with a two-acre pond on it. They had horses and dogs, as well as an assortment of other fury residents.

Animal lovers to be sure. I called them on a whim and laid out my dilemma. "Sure, we'd love to have them," she said. It sounded like music to my ears. "We have one lonely goose here already. She hangs out with the wild Canada geese during the day, but they leave in the afternoon and then she's left all alone. When did you want to bring them?" The question caught me off guard.

"Ah, I'm not sure, can I call you back?"

"Of course, just let us know, anytime will be fine."

That all happened too fast, and I guess I needed a bit of time to wrap my mind around letting them go. As annoying and inconvenient as they were, I had gotten awfully attached and was feeling a real pull in my spirit when I hung up the phone. Our anniversary was two weeks away, that would be a nice present for Sharon I thought. I'll take them then. When Sharon came home, I told her I found the perfect place for the geese; I don't know how I didn't think of it sooner. The relief on Sharon's face was obvious.

When the day came, I put the cap on my old pickup and filled the bed with mulch so they'd have a comfortable ride. The drive was about two hours away and Sharon surprised me by taking the day off so she could ride along. The geese took it as a personal affront to be unceremoniously picked up and dumped in the back of a truck and they let me know in no uncertain terms it was beneath their dignity.

When we pulled out of the driveway, I looked in the rear-view mirror and saw all their little heads together only inches apart and for the first time ever they were silent. That all changed when we hit the highway and passed our first transfer truck. They exploded in a chorus of screams that silenced the roar of eighteen wheels and a diesel engine.

They were a bunch of country bumpkins on their first trip off the farm. Everything was new. The motion of the ride, the noises, the open space outside their window. What a shock it must have been.

When we arrived, I drove down a gravel driveway that led to the pond and backed up as close to the water as I could get. What a perfect spot! Big open water surrounded by delicious green grass, their favorite food. So much better than their pathetic little plastic blue Walmart kiddie pool in the driveway at home.

There were about fifty wild geese at the far end of the pond quite a distance away, but I was curious to see how they would react. I really was excited for them. We got out of the truck, walked around and opened the tail gate, and swung the cap door open. I expected

Clarence the goose.

Sharon's geese

them to rush out and make a beeline for the pond but they didn't move. Didn't make a sound. I climbed in the back and pushed them out one by one then climbed back out myself. They all clung around my ankles. If I moved, they all moved in unison. They were terrified. I ushered them down to the pond and had to push Clarence in the water, but the second he couldn't feel his feet touch the bottom, he panicked and shot back out faster than I've ever seen him move.

I tried to get them all in at once figuring they'd feel safer. That was not happening either.

Thaddeus saw the gravel road and it must have looked familiar to him because he gave the call and they all started walking towards the road, probably believing it would lead home. They were having none of this. I called to them but they wouldn't come so I ran around and got in front and tried to herd the flock back to the water. They stopped by the truck and refused to go any further, so I sat down in the grass with them—that delicious fresh green grass. I pulled some up and tried to make a peace offering. Nope. They headed back to the road. I rounded them back up and pointed them in the direction of the water.

A flock of about thirty wild geese flew into view, all noisy and calling, coming in for a landing.

Our geese stopped and stood rigid, watching. When they landed, the wild geese already there got excited and started calling, their voices joining with the new comers. What a racket! Our geese were mortified. These were obviously "super geese"! How could they ever compete?

The resident pet goose heard the commotion and flew in just over our heads to join in the melee with the locals. They all huddled around Sharon and I, looking very concerned. We sat there with them for close to an hour hoping they would calm down and feel comfortable. But it wasn't going to happen. It was all just too much for them. There was no pen or building to leave them in to get used to the place and start to feel at home. It was obvious that as soon as we left, they would start walking up the road looking for home. Even though the property was fenced, it was not a fence that would hold geese, and besides the gates were all open. I was sure they would just keep walking, looking for home, and probably end up on a busy road or worse.

Sharon had been watching this whole scene play out and drew her own conclusions. She walked over to me, tears streaming down her cheeks and her face contorted from trying not to burst out crying. "We can't leave them here!" she wailed. "They've never known any place but ours, they're scared and they'll never be happy

heeeeeeeeere." She threw her arm my neck sobbing. The geese had (were obviously in total agreemen was finally able to gather herself to in the truck and let's go home. I'll

That's my wife. Sharon. Eve Even the feelings of a goose. So, e home. There is goose poop ever weapons handy and a little blue V also with goose poop in it.

Nothing much has changed, e: "Rob's geese," they're "Sharon's g

The geese in their

Don't Ignore the Small Things

When she first came to us, she was no bigger than my thumb. A helpless, hungry, furry being who lived in darkness and silence. Neither her ears nor her eyes had opened yet. Like all babies, her existence was nothing more than eating, sleeping, and feeling the pain of hunger; perhaps the gentle touch and smell of mother. She could drink no more than one cc of formula every four hours so getting up a couple of times during the night those first couple of weeks was necessary.

A cat had found her among the leaves on the forest floor and brought the prize home as a gift.

Thankfully she was not harmed and a compassionate man brought her to us believing her chances of survival were slim at best. I too, had reservations about our ability to help something so small and fragile. But in her world, nothing much had changed. It was still dark and it was quiet; a heating pad was placed under her box so she remained warm, and as long as the food kept coming, she was content.

When she was a little over a month old her eyes began to open, her fur was soft and luxurious and her tail had started to fluff up a bit with many fine feather-like hairs. By seven weeks she was becoming curious about the world outside of her nest box and like all nocturnal creatures was most active at night.

She is a southern flying squirrel. We are very familiar with them, they come to our bird feeder at night by the dozen. Like frantic lunatics, jazzed up and reckless on a caffeine induced frenzy, gliding in from all directions on invisible zip lines to inundate the feeding station with constant motion. Unusually tame and trusting, they occasionally allow us to touch their unbelievably soft fur with a slow-moving finger. I was confident we would be able to gradually introduce and release her into this local tribe and all would be well.

The first feelings of reluctance started to emerge when my wife gave her a name: Florence, 'Flo' for short. Before long I had allowed myself to be drawn in and swallowed up by her large, sorrowful, and almost cartoon-like eyes. As she grew and her personality emerged it became impossible to resist her. If she heard us in the living room, she would bound out of her box, grab the bars of her cage, and shake them like an enraged prisoner. I could envision her dragging a miniature tin cup back and forth across the bars and pleading to the warden for release. When I open the door and put my hand in her cage she jumps into my palm, takes her tiny hands, wraps them around a finger, and presses her soft little head against the skin in an obvious affectionate hug. This, of course, causes my heart to completely unravel and I immediately find a thousand reasons why she can never be released into the wild.

The TV has become obsolete now, as our evenings are taken up by the most entertaining and lively companion. It seems she can never decide who she loves more as she bounds back and forth between my wife and I, dancing up a pant leg or shirt sleeve, finding a cozy pocket or a snuggle spot. If you're lying down, she loves to lie across your throat so she can feel the vibration when you speak to her. She loves games and insists we participate. Hide and seek being her favorite, of course.

There are blinds made from a honeycombed fabric that hang from all our windows she speeds up, down, and across, chasing or being chased by a flagitious finger and squeaks her annoyance if you don't let her win. She likes to sample whatever you may be snacking on (thank you very much) and can literally attach herself to your face to pry loose anything from your lips you foolishly try to hoard for yourself. She even likes to partake in a little snort of blueberry beer— just to be social you understand.

A gregarious socialite, Flo loves to meet new people and will wake up during the day if there are visitors. She's never as lively during the daylight hours but simply must come out to introduce herself and greet the guests.

Less than ten inches from the tip of her nose to the end of her tail, smaller than a chipmunk, but her personality fills the room. An orphaned fox squirrel was brought to us several weeks after Flo. He was a lumbering, slow-witted giant by comparison with a distinct personality of his own, but could never match the swift antics of his smaller cousin.

Sometimes nature finds her fairest expression in such small living things. As a casual observer, a naturalist, even as a scientist, we miss out on the most intimate details of life when we ignore or gloss over the possibilities of relationship. And who would imagine becoming so fond of the tiny whiskered face of a rodent, the sharp wit and sensitivity behind those dark eyes; no longer a mystery, but a portal into a new level of understanding. Being raised by people has made her unafraid, but it hasn't made her less intelligent, less curious, social, or mischievous. I watch the behavior of her cousins that visit our feeder at night. They are the same, fun-loving socialites with a contagious exuberance.

So, when the first warm breath of spring blows through the forest, just a few months from now, Flo will move to a cage out on the back deck by the feeding station where she can start to have relationship with her new tribe. The research I've done on these tiny nocturnal acrobats is not encouraging. Most don't make it through their first year. Owls, weasels, hawks, and snakes work against their odds; even so, she deserves the chance to become a mother and help perpetuate her kind.

Even if her dance is short, it will have purpose and no doubt, great enthusiasm.

Flo at six weeks old.

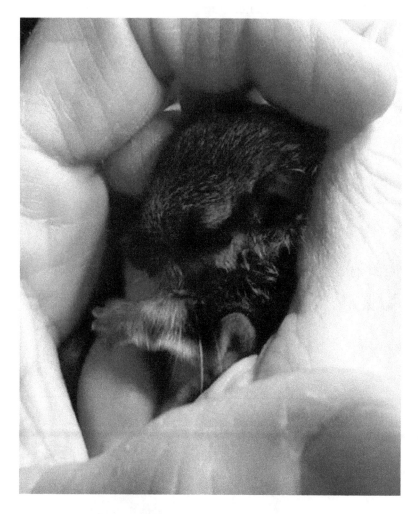

Flo at twelve weeks old

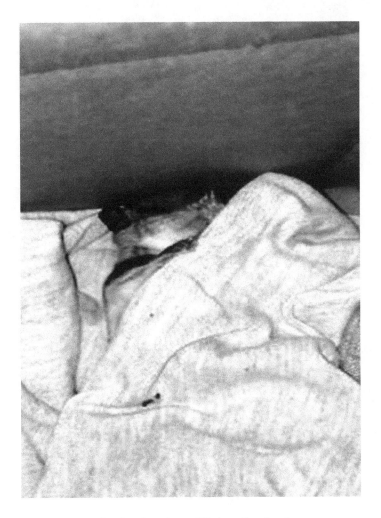

Flo the Southern Flying Squirrel

Flo as an adult.

Woody the Squirrel

We have squirrels. I can't help but feel that may be an understatement. We have very many squirrels. Not hundreds, but at times it can feel that way. You see, I've been fighting a losing battle against these birdseed-eating hordes since we moved here eight years ago. While I have gained a healthy respect for their abilities to thwart any schemes designed to prevent their gluttonous consumption of our avian guest's meals, my disdain for their presence has reached epic proportions.

Recently I've been reconsidering my "live in harmony with all creatures" stance and have considered "violence leading to eradication" as an alternate mission statement. I am convinced that if squirrels were human they would be nuclear physicists, mathematicians, engineers, or some form of demented evil genius. They are unrelenting and goal oriented. As humans, they would all be billionaires. None of these statements are in question for anyone who has had to deal with these rodents on a regular basis.

Squirrel guards, squirrel-proof feeders (what a joke), sending my dogs after them (they never get close), air horns to frighten them, even throwing cold water on them makes not the slightest difference. They just keep coming. They poop and pee and chew on our deck. If the feeder is empty, they chew on our vinyl windows. Every morning,

I walk out to fill the feeder as many as a dozen squirrels scatter in all directions. It's gotten out of hand. I'll just go ahead and say it—I despise them. I had decided to take matters in another direction, one that lined up with my latter mission statement.

That is, until my daughter called.

"Dad, I found a baby squirrel at the side of the road. He has a puncture wound in his chest and one eye looks cloudy and infected. What should I do? Will you take him?"

Karma is a persistent guest in my life.

My daughter is too naive to be perverse in her naming of this young male squirrel.

"Woody" has been with us now for about six weeks.

He lived with us in our house for the first few weeks until he was healed up and no longer drinking the expensive powdered goats milk formula.

We have a pair of southern flying squirrels that came to us as babies. They live in a large outdoor habitat and can't be released because they have imprinted on people, are very tame, and probably wouldn't survive in the wild. I moved "Greg and Flo" to a smaller enclosure and moved Woody into their home. It was a temporary arrangement. Just until I could drop several hundred dollars building Woody a habitat of his own. Karma can be costly.

Over the years I've had the privilege of raising or rehabilitating hundreds of wild animals.

But never a gray squirrel.

When you take the time to develop a relationship with a wild animal, you are given the unique opportunity to see another side of their personality. Often, intimate details that could never be gathered even from hundreds of hours of observation in fieldwork.

The other day, I was spending some time with Carl the crow. Another resident with an aviary just a few feet from Woody's home. There is a chair in Carl's cage where I sit while visiting. He requires copious amounts of intellectual stimulation (games he designed for me to lose) so visits are not allowed to be short. I looked over just as Woody had jumped up on a stump with arms full of leaves.

Once perched on the stump he threw the leaves in the air then, as they fell, quickly grabbed as many as he could catch and pull them back into his chest and belly. He flopped over on his back and once again threw the leaves into the air. This was done with such obvious joy and abandon that I couldn't help but be moved. His joy became my joy and I laughed out loud.

I have been watching squirrels all my life, I've never seen one do that! I'm not saying they don't, but an animal in the wild, particularly one that low on the food chain, is always on the lookout for enemies. The question I would ask is, do they even possess the freedom or peace of mind (in the wild) to experience that kind of pure uninterrupted joy?

My answer to that question would be: Of course they do. Woody just proved it. Just because I've never observed it doesn't mean it doesn't happen. The knowledge of my presence alone would prevent it in the wild. Unless a wild squirrel was as comfortable with me as Woody is.

And trust me, around here, they are not.

So, Woody has become family. My wife and I spend as much time with him as we can. He is curious and playful and very lovable. Not like the seed-eating hordes that flow from the surrounding forest like Attila and all the Huns, seeking out our bird feeders, leaving their detestable excrement and destructive chewing habits in their wake.

Woody is soft and cuddly, like a "Tickle Me Elmo" doll. He will jump from a branch onto your shoulder, stick his nose in your ear, and grunt soft little sounds. He'll run down your arm, grab a couple of your fingers, gather them up to his chest and gently nibble while grunting. He'll roll over on his back in the palm of your hand and wait to be tickled on his exposed belly. Then he tries to push your finger away and turns his head from side to side, just like you were tickling a small child.

Needless to say, we are quite fond of Woody.

My wife and I worked for several days on a new squirrel habitat for Woody. When moving day arrived and everything was in place, I wondered how best to move him. Over the years I've become overconfident or maybe cavalier in my assessment of how animals should be handled.

Woody jumped on my shoulder when I walked in his enclosure. I thought, no need to stress him out by putting him in a box. His new home is only forty feet away, I'll just walk him over on my shoulder.

Even an amateur should have known better.

Twenty feet from the cage, our dog walked over to me for a greeting. Woody was spooked and jumped from my shoulder and landed on the driveway, terrified. He dashed over to Carl's cage and ran up the side. Carl wasted no time and in a flash was after the squirrel. Woody leapt from the cage and landed on the forest floor with a thud. At that moment he looked just like any other squirrel that needed chasing. Our dog seized the opportunity and was in hot pursuit.

Woody leapt for the nearest tree and scrambled to the tipper most top, fifty feet off the ground.

This happened to be the coldest and windiest day of the late fall season. Woody, now perched on little more than twigs in the top of an oak tree, swayed back and forth as the wind pushed the forest canopy in all directions.

I felt like an idiot. Which in fact, I was. My wife confirmed that assessment, and concurred with all my verbal debasements of my personhood that followed. When I was done, she turned and walked towards the house.

"Where are you going?" I asked

"In the house to get a blanket?"

"Why?"

She stopped and turned to face the idiot.

"Because it's cold outside, and I'm going to sit in a chair by that tree, all day if necessary, and wait for him to come down."

It was 8:30 a.m.

By 5 o'clock it was getting dark, and Woody had moved only slightly (and not in a downward motion) in over eight hours. We were so cold and our necks were sore and stiff from looking up all day. It was time to give up our vigil for the day. The wind had died down somewhat but the temperature was dropping fast. Clinging to the top branches exposed like he was, Woody would be easy prey for an owl tonight. Even if an owl didn't find him, I felt exposure to the cold could very well do him in. He hadn't had time to develop a thick winter coat like the wild squirrels had and because of his previous injuries his growth was a little stunted. He was smaller than the other squirrels and weaker.

Sharon went in the house to make us something to eat and I stayed outside a few more minutes waiting. At 5:30 I walked towards the house. Standing on the porch, I turned back for one last look.

A small silhouette was making its way down the trunk of that tree. It was almost dark now and I could barely make out his movements. I ran in the house for a flashlight and Sharon followed me back outside. We spent the next half hour looking for Woody. We combed the forest floor, looked up the surrounding trees with our flashlights, and scanned a perimeter larger than probably necessary. But we never found him.

Visions of a little Woody curled up on the forest floor shivering, hungry, thirsty, and scared made sleep impossible. At 6 a.m. the following morning I headed back outside. I thought I would just sit in the chair and as it started to get light, I would wait for movement in the leaves. With any luck at all I would find him.

I had left the door of his cage open just in case, and when I approached the chair, something shot out from the leaves and hit the inside wire of the cage startling me. I shone the flashlight into the cage and there sat Woody. But only for a second. He was not accustomed to being awake when it was dark, nor was he used to the intense beam from a flashlight. He dove into his nest box faster than my eye could follow, then poked his head out for reassurance. I spoke his name and when he heard my voice, he started to shake all over, then disappeared back into his box. I decided to shut the door and let him rest. I would check on him later. But when I went in the house to tell Sharon, she had to get up and see for herself. The wave of relief that washed over the two of us was not surprising. Nor has the irony of being happy to see a squirrel been lost on me.

We took the necessary precautions and moved Woody several days later to his new home, where he seems very content. Now, however, it was time to move the flying squirrels back to their own cage.

This would be much more involved. We often refer to the flying squirrel habitat as "Hotel California" because you can come in but you can never leave. They are like two meth addicts jazzed up on a caffeine frenzy. They never stop moving. In your pocket one minute then down your shirt and out your shirt sleeves the next. Jumping from branch to branch then on to your head and down your back, around your leg and back up to your face, quicker than the human eye can follow. Every time you think you can make your escape and head out the door, they are on you again. Quite comical and entertaining, until you've been trapped for over half an hour waiting for an opportunity to escape while being used as a human trampoline. Their move did not go as planned either... but that's another story.

Woody the Squirrel.

A Crow Named Eddie

A friend of ours called late one afternoon. "There's a large black bird in a tree by our house. It's in the lower branches and doesn't seem to be afraid. Do you think it could be sick? It's been there for a couple hours and hasn't moved."

When we arrived, a family of crows was hanging about all in a tizzy. Obviously, something had upset them, their jittery flights from tree to tree and the constant calling back and forth told me a problem had presented itself and they were dealing with it the way crows do.

When I approached the tree, I saw a young crow sitting very still far out on a low limb. Old enough to fly, but still in need of feeding from his parents. Normally, approaching a young crow like this would bring about the wrath of its parents, swooping low and creating a ruckus in an effort to drive away any perceived threat to their young. But the crows became strangely quiet as I drew closer and just as our friend had said, the young bird seemed unafraid of my presence. I stood beside him and talked softly as we were now face to face. There was hardly any reaction.

His feathers were not puffed up, his eyes were the soft blue color of a juvenile, but bright and clear. He was just oddly calm.

Even more unusual, was the reaction of the crows in the trees overhead. Not a sound or movement came from their direction. Oh, they were very interested in what was taking place, but were playing no role in the outcome. I found the situation unsettling. I am very familiar with crows and never encountered anything like this before. I reached up and touched the young bird, ran my finger over his head, down his neck and across his back. No reaction.

Something was very wrong, the whole setting was off, nothing was behaving as it should.

I noticed some areas around its head that looked like feathers had been pulled out. I thought he behaved as though he had been attacked or roughed up a bit. Were the parents trying to drive him away? Were these crows even his parents? Had he somehow wandered into another pair's territory and they were reacting to an intruder? Young crows don't mate until they are three or four years old and will stay in the area and help raise and protect the offspring of other crows.

I had no way of knowing for sure but my sense was that these birds overhead were his parents, the others were his siblings, and for whatever reason they no longer wanted him around. I picked him up and placed him in a box we had brought along.

There was no resistance from him and no reaction from the crows in the trees above.

At home, I tried offering some food, but there was no interest. I decided to leave him till the morning and try again. When morning arrived, he was still refusing food and still had no reaction to my presence. I wondered if he had a brain injury or some other physical injury I had overlooked. I gave him a thorough exam and found nothing out of place. I force-fed him some meat and he took it down without much resistance.

Within a couple of days, he was taking food from my fingers, but still his behavior was odd.

Other crows I had raised were curious and playful, their fine intellect obvious even at a young age. Corvids have unusually large brains for their size and are well known for their intelligence.

They have been observed making and using tools as well as having the ability to count. Their communication skills are also well documented. A crow will remember the face of someone who has tried to hurt it and will communicate the information to other crows.

This strange little orphan displayed no emotion whatsoever. I moved his cage out on the front porch during the day and sat with him for short periods of time, but there was not much of a reaction to me, our dogs, or the wild birds that came by our feeder. He just sat on a branch in his cage. I wondered if he was depressed, but it wasn't that, it was something else.

Over the next couple of weeks, he did perk up a bit and I had a small insight into his personality. We had plans to visit our daughter in South Korea so I asked our friend Ashley, if she would take care of "Eddie" while we were gone. (I don't remember how Eddie came by his name.) After we had been gone for about a week, I received a message from Ashley that Eddie was sick and had developed a large tumor-like growth on the inside of his top bill. She sent along pictures, but it was nothing I could identify. She took him to a local wildlife rehabilitator who tried to lance the growth with a scalpel. Much to the discomfort of poor Eddie.

By the time we arrived home, the growth had started to deform the upper bill. Eddie seemed pleased to see me, it was the first time I saw him display any emotion. We sat on the porch together, and I feed him little treats of meat and blueberries while he perched on my leg and cuddled in close to my body, obviously content and relaxed.

The next day I took him to a veterinarian who specialized in birds, but she really had no clue as to what caused the growth or how to treat it. She sent us home with a foul-tasting antibiotic that I had to force-feed poor Eddie twice daily. After two weeks of treatment the growth had become so large it was difficult for Eddie to swallow his food.

By now, of course, we were attached to Eddie and naturally felt responsible for him. My wife searched the internet for his symptoms. Within minutes she had a diagnosis. Avian Pox! His parents knew weeks ago there was something wrong with this nestling and drove him off in an effort to protect the family.

Avian Pox is highly contagious to other birds. Mosquitoes, mites, midges, flies, and fleas are culprits in transmitting the disease. These insects pick up the virus when they bite an infected host then transmit the virus when they bite another. The virus can also be transmitted when they are in direct contact with an infected bird, or infected objects like bird feeders. There really wasn't any treatment. The disease had to run its course. The antibiotic was good for treating any secondary infection of the lesion or growth on his upper bill, but could do nothing for the disease. Many wild birds that become infected die when lesions grow around their eyes or nostrils, affecting their eyesight or breathing. Others can even lose toes or feet if the infection is bad enough in that area. The poultry industry vaccinates against avian pox, but wild birds are on their own.

At least now we had some answers and an understanding of his odd behavior. Eddie had been sick since we brought him home and was only now showing outward signs of a serious virus. There would be no more sitting outside where the chance of spreading something so contagious was possible. Eddie was in quarantine till things improved.

Finally, after several weeks, the tumor-like growth started to shrink. Every day saw a noticeable improvement. At its peak it was the size of a marble, now reduced to the size of a pea. Eddie was feeling much better as well. He was getting restless in that cage and was ready to get out and do some damage in ways that only a crow can conceive. He was also becoming affectionate. He loved to have his neck and ears scratched, would perch on my shoulder and pull gently on my ears or hair. He gurgled and gargled and make soft cooing sounds when he saw me and for fun would try to pinch the dogs' tails when they walked by him. Occasionally, Eddie would get knocked off his perch by a wagging tail. This, of course, required immediate retribution and it was "game on" with Gus and Gertie our two German Shepherds.

The sun room, (where Eddie's cage was kept) was starting to smell a little too funky for Sharon, so plans were drawn up for a large outside aviary. Up till this point he never showed any desire to fly, he just hopped around the house finding trouble where he could. Eventually Eddie would be given a free ride back to his cage so the other residents of our home could secure a little peace and quiet. He had come to life and was discovering himself. And it seemed, he rather liked himself.

The growth had almost disappeared completely, but his upper bill was left slightly deformed.

The curve was a little exaggerated with a slight hump and a bit offset from the lower mandible. Not that he allowed that to slow him down in anyway. His behavior now was more like the behavior of crows I had raised in the past. Playful, cunning, mischievous, brave, extremely intelligent and of course, arrogant. But there were other aspects of his personality that were different. He just seemed a little off his game somehow. He tired easily and was more affectionate than other corvids I've raised. I started to refer to Eddie as a "she" because I just had a feeling. Eddie never "cawed" like other crows. Mostly she just made little growling sounds, like somebody that was irritated, mumbling under their breath. Or when she was in the mood, content maybe, she would sit on my shoulder and make soft, musical sounds in my ear. The comment was made more than once that she was ugly. It was true she was not a fine example of a crow. Her beak was humped and crooked, no matter how often she bathed her feathers remained dull looking, and she was a bit smaller than normal. But what she lacked in beauty was more than compensated for in her personality.

My friend Phillip came over one afternoon and we spent several hours constructing a sizable aviary for Eddie. It was midsummer in North Carolina and Eddie needed her own space outside.

She took to it immediately. Checking out all the possible hiding spots for her stashes of items she determined had value. These were usually made up of the sort of things she was able to steal from reluctant human benefactors. The harder it was to steal, the more value was placed on the item. I put a chair in the cage so I could sit with her and hang out when I had time. She loved being the center of attention and would at times reveal to me her secret stashes and the ill-gotten gains they contained. This was a particular source of pride for her, and while I was allowed to look, admire, and make a fuss over her treasures, I was never allowed to touch them.

Her new home was built right outside the kitchen window so we could always keep an eye on her. One day I looked out just in time to see a Cooper's hawk slam into the side of her cage, hitting the wire from a full-on attack and bounce off stunned. Rather than retreat, Eddie threw herself up against the wire from the inside and tried to get at the hapless predator for a revenge strike. The groggy hawk took a couple of drunken shaky steps and stood there trying to regain its composure. When I stepped outside it flew away. Eddie came dancing over like an excited kid who had just bested the school yard bully in a standoff. I went in and sat with her awhile so she could tell me all about it. I was concerned she would no longer feel safe in her new home, but rather than feel like a targeted victim, the incident left her feeling like a boss. She now officially "owned" her space and was only too eager to show our dogs who was in charge. When they came close enough to the chicken wire, she stuck her beak through for a quick "pinch and run."

My wife and I had bought some property in the Blue Ridge mountains of Virginia and over the years built a small log house in the woods to use as a retreat. We later named the property "The Woodlands of Ivor" in honor of Roy Ivor, a Canadian ornithologist and naturalist I had worked with as a boy. We decided to go up and stay for the weekend, so I asked a friend to look in on Eddie while we were away. When we came home the following Monday, Eddie didn't look well. She was all puffed up, eyes half closing and a little wobbly on her perch. I was very concerned and called my friend to see if anything had happened while we were away. He was confident all was well, but I wasn't really sure he knew what to look out for.

I thought about taking her to the vet, but putting her in a box and driving her to the vet only to be poked and prodded would be too stressful in her present condition. Besides, I had lost confidence in a vet who couldn't diagnose a common disease like avian pox.

Fortunately, by the end of the day Eddie had perked up somewhat and was looking and acting more like herself. It took a couple more days for her to fully recover from whatever it was, but recover she did. A couple weeks later when we went back to our place in Virginia, we took Eddie with us. She traveled like a boss in the back seat with our dogs Gus and Gertie and upon arrival had to make a thorough examination of the premises to be sure it met with her standards. A good selection of places to stash ill-gotten gains? Check. Furniture that has yet to be pooped on? Check. Rob and Sharon, here to provide tasty meals and clean water for drinking and bathing? Check. Dogs that will provide me with entertaining victims to harass and torment?

Excellent! Everything seems to be in order.

This, however, was not going to be a weekend where only Eddie had fun at everyone else's expense. Which, of course, would have been just fine with her. Eddie was watching me from inside the house peering out an open living room window when I pulled her cage out from the back of Sharon's Honda Element. If a bird is capable of having a look of "horror" on their face, I was sure I detected one the second before she disappeared from view. I was not in the mood for a game of hide and seek, so I left the cage on the front porch and walked in the house like I had no plans of a nefarious nature for Eddie's future. I've been involved in a battle of wits with corvids many times over the years and there's a fifty percent chance I come out on the losing end of any contest. The one thing I had going in my favor with this particular corvid was that she didn't fly and could be easily caught once she revealed herself. But what I've learned—and it's an important lesson—the only way to truly win in a contest with a crow or a raven is to do it in such a way that the bird thinks it has actually won. In this way you can be certain there will be no retaliatory schemes cooked up by these avian geniuses at a later time when you're least expecting it.

I picked up a small rock and made a huge fuss over it while Sharon quietly set up her cage with food and water and her favorite little stump of wood to perch on. Eddie came out of hiding to see what I was so excited about. Naturally she had to have this precious object and came for it with enthusiasm. But I wouldn't let her have it. Not yet.

I took some string and wrapped it around and around the stone while Eddie watched. Then I took a sheet of paper and gift wrapped the string covered stone and for good measure, wrapped string around the paper covering the stone. By this time Eddie was beside herself with anticipation. The thought of stealing something that I took so much time and care with . . . well, it was just beyond her ability to resist any longer. For the first time ever, Eddie flew to my hand and tried to grab the treasure from my fingers. This surprised and delighted us both, but her distraction lasted less than a millisecond. Her crooked little beak had a grip on her prize and she was determined to have it. I pulled it away, walked outside and pretended to hide it in her cage.

Eddie pretended not to notice, but when I stepped away, she hopped into the cage and quickly retrieved her reward. I closed the door but she was too distracted to notice. She spent the next half hour on her little wood stump unwrapping and unraveling her stone with a determined glee.

The rest of us settled in and relaxed.

It was early in the evening; the sun had set but it was still light outside. Sharon and I were finishing up our supper when Eddie started screaming a blood curdling caaaaawww, caaaaawwww, caaaawww. (Something else she had never done before.) I jumped up from my chair and ran outside sure that something terrible was happening to her. She continued her alarming cries even when I stood beside her cage. I could see nothing wrong with her, but movement in a tree beside the porch caught my eye. I looked up and saw a huge great horned owl perched in a branch looking down on what he thought was going to be an easy meal. Eddie had never seen an owl before but knew instinctively this was real danger.

Great horned owls are a crow's worst enemy. They can come into a flock of roosting crows at night when they are defenseless and pick off any they choose for a quick dinner. During the daylight hours, if a crow finds a roosting owl, he sends forth the alarm in much the same way Eddie was doing now, alerting any crows within earshot. Soon ten, twenty, as many as a hundred crows or more come in from all directions to mob and torment the hapless creature. They "count coup" by diving in to get as close as possible. The bravest among them getting in a solid peck to the head or pulling out a feather. Eventually, the owl will try to flee its tormentors by flying off, but not without a multitude of black assassins in tow all screaming in a particular tone reserved for this one act. They do the same to hawks on occasion but it's never done with the same relentless fervor or at the same decibel level as with great horned owls. Eventually, the mob grows bored and they move on to fight another day. Rarely, if ever, is the owl seriously injured.

This owl did not appreciate my presence and flew into the forest to seek out another opportunity. The empty branch didn't pacify Eddie much and she continued her alarm calls for another five minutes before finally settling down for the evening.

Over the course of the next year or so we had to leave Eddie in the care of a friend when we were away on weekend retreats with our youth group or family visits out of town. Each time we returned home to find her in a sickly state, and just like that first time, she would take several days to recover. A pattern had developed. I suspected she just became depressed when her friend was gone and her routine changed. I also felt that the sickness she had when young was serious enough to have left her in a weakened state and possibly a weakened immune system.

To the casual observer Eddie seemed like just another crow, but I could see she just wasn't as robust as a normal crow. She tired easily and never would have survived in the wild. A predator would be alert and keenly aware of her disability in seconds, picking up on subtle clues that would be obvious to the trained eye of a hungry opportunist.

When I have written about crows or ravens I've raised in the past, I almost feel I could be writing about the same bird, because their personalities are so similar. Every species of animal, including humans, display certain characteristics and behaviors that are predictable and common. Maybe, this is why we find it so easy to generalize people of another race or nationality. When we allow ourselves the opportunity to know the individual, we learn things that change our minds and enlighten us in ways that better our understanding of ourselves and the whole human race. The same is true with animals. Only when you develop a relationship, can you get a glimpse of the individual and see the differences.

If Eddie was human, I would have admired her for her sharp intellect and wonderful sense of humor. She was easy to love because she loved me, accepted my person unconditionally and found pleasure in my company. Who wouldn't enjoy a friend like this?

In April of 2012, we sold our home in North Carolina and moved full time to the Woodlands of Ivor. Our retreat became our home. I looked forward to taking on more animals for rehabilitation now that we had the land and privacy we needed. I had hoped that I could begin to let Eddie out for long periods of time during the day when I was close by and maybe she could build up her strength and endurance. But she showed no desire to leave her aviary unless it was to come in the house and hang with her "buds."

Our daughter returned home from South Korea and lived with us for a few months. She and Eddie became fast friends. Sometimes, Virginia would take a book and sit with Eddie in her cage and read. That would never have been possible for me, she would have been tearing at the book or harassing me in some other way to assure that she had my undivided attention. But with Virginia, she seemed content just to have her company and left her in peace. Maybe just untying a shoelace or "tasting" buttons on her shirt. Eddie liked Virginia. But really, Eddie liked everyone. She wasn't as assertive as other corvids I've raised and as a rule she got along well with strangers.

In July, Sharon and I had to leave once again to attend a three-day seminar in Pennsylvania.

Our son and his wife lived close by at the time so he took care of all the animals while we were away. I talked with him daily, checking in on how everyone was doing and he assured us all was well. When we returned home, once again Eddie was sickly. I walked into her aviary and could tell she was relieved to see me, but could hardly muster up the strength to give me a proper greeting. She perched on my thigh and leaned in close to my body, puffed up and a little unsteady. We sat together until dusk. I hated to leave her for the night but was hoping she would follow her usual routine and by the next day would start to improve. She didn't improve. I thought about driving her to the wildlife rehabilitation center in Waynesboro where a qualified veterinarian could examine her, but in my heart, I knew it was already too late. The stress would have been too much for her anyway. By the following morning she was dead.

"Little Eddie" wasn't "just" a crow, any more than our dog is "just" a dog. Relationship changes everything. Anyone who has ever loved a dog and sees a dog lying dead at the side of the road will feel differently than a person who has never had a dog as a member of their family or as a best friend. Intimacy and relationship with an animal, wild or domestic, is a portal into which we fall, only to come out on the other side drenched in knowledge that we wouldn't otherwise be privileged to possess. There is no animal I see and think, 'oh, it's just a . . .' I've had the privilege of relationship with so many animals over the years, I have a clear understanding of the possibilities that exist.

Sometimes people inhabit their bodies without valuing themselves, unable to see that the here and now, this very moment is sacred. But once it's gone, its value is uncontested. I don't believe animals live anywhere but in the moment. Their lives may be shorter, but because of this, perhaps fuller.

I also understand that once nature has made a decision, she seldom changes her mind. In the end, all I could do for Eddie was prolong the inevitable. That time was a gift for both of us. And of Eddie, there is no more to tell.

Eddie the Crow

Apples for Monica

Thaddeus, Clarence, Iris and, Monica are the names we've given to four geese that spend their days navigating the woods that surround our home. It's not a natural environment for geese. One would assume they would prefer a more open space with thick, delicious green grass to eat and perhaps a pond to play and bathe in. But no. We once tried to re-home them in such a place and they would have none of it. They are content with the Walmart kiddie pool made from blue plastic and the small overgrazed areas of lawn around our house. They patrol the grounds like small dinosaurs, completely confident in their authority and look with disdain upon all others who must share their space.

Nothing escapes their notice. Even at night. We are often awakened very late, when a raccoon, opossum, or some other nocturnal neighbor has the audacity to wander too close. The alarm is sounded and no one within a half mile of our residence is unaware that something has disturbed them.

Each one has a distinct personality. Whenever you see them, they are together and always at least one of them is on guard and watching for danger. Except Monica. She lives in her own world.

Usually lagging behind seemingly lost in thought. She has a quiet and gentle demeanor.

There is a softness in her eyes and unlike the others' ear-splitting screams, honking, and incessant chatter, she has a voice like cascading laughter.

Often Monica gets left behind. While the others are methodically grazing and moving on to the side or back of the house, Monica seems to be daydreaming. Suddenly waking to find she's been deserted by the others who were so involved with eating they hadn't noticed she was gone.

Sometimes if they're in the mood, they'll follow the dogs and I up the driveway rocking side by side on stubby little legs and chatting continuously. We stop at the "peace garden" where a couple of chairs have been reserved for my wife and I to sit and take in the beauty surrounding us. If my wife is with me, they have to stay behind as they share a mutual disdain for each other.

To be fair, the geese have a disdain for everyone but me. However, given the right circumstances, they have been known to take the odd swipe when my back is turned. This is a recent development and I've yet to understand what prompts this behavior other than a goose's surly and "dickish" attitude towards all non-goose life forms.

Once I'm seated and comfortable, they all gather around conversing in light chatter about God knows what. They get as close as they can and untie my shoelaces or pull on my pant legs.

Except Monica. Since she was very small, she has had a fascination with my wedding band.

Very quietly, she pushes past the others and gently at first, nibbles on the gold metal. Her bill sounds like chattering teeth as she tastes the edges of the band. Unfortunately, the gentle nibbles quickly escalate into a wrenching tug of war as she tries to pull the band from my finger.

If her bill slips off the ring, my finger gets pinched with such gusto it feels like it's caught in a steel trap. When I pull my hand away and shout at her to stop, she genuinely looks surprised and maybe even a little sad that she hurt me. However, she just can't resist that ring and within seconds is back softly nibbling, looking up at me as if to ask, "Is this okay, I'm not hurting you now, am I?"

Their little "gaggle" is fun to watch. They are very loyal to one another and show genuine concern if they notice Monica is not among them. When migrating wild geese have a member of the flock that has been injured, some may stay behind until it dies or can rejoin the flock. Geese can live a long time, up to thirty years in captivity. Wild geese don't live as long, most are killed in their first year by a predator.

Geese love to eat grass, but also partake in nuts and berries as well as insects. Ours prefer whatever we're growing in our gardens. Except Monica. More than anything else, more than grass, more than garden greens, more even than my wedding band, Monica loves apples! The only time you'll ever see Monica in a hurry is when she knows you have an apple.

She is somewhat of a connoisseur as well. She knows the difference between a Gala and Red Delicious. Granny apples and Golden Delicious are "Ho hum" and Macintosh are a bit tart for her taste. Fuji apples are her favorite. (I had to pause for a moment after I wrote that to consider what kind of person takes the time to learn the kinds of apples a goose likes, but then decided it would be best not to dwell too long on my occasional nerd-like behavior and attention to details pertaining to animal behavior.) I even save my apple cores and give them to Monica.

She appreciates my thoughtfulness.

I was concerned for their lives the first winter we had them. It became so cold and the thermometer on the front porch dropped down into the single digits. I built them a little house and filled it with soft comfy straw. But they would never go inside. There could be a blizzard with thirty mile an hour winds and bitter cold, but they would just sit there, slowly disappearing under a blanket of snow.

Last winter when we had two weeks of unusual cold, I physically picked them up and put them in the house, then nailed a piece of wood to the doorway so they couldn't leave. As it turns out, it wasn't necessary. The large flat feet of waterfowl are natural radiators; the arteries and veins in a goose's legs work in tandem to retain heat. They are also covered in dense layers of feather down that is most efficient holding in body heat. This winter they are on their own . . . maybe.

A friend of mine visited the other day. When he got out of his car, he was immediately surrounded and accosted by this local band of thugs. He had to walk backwards bent down with his hands in front of him vigorously defending his lower extremities. When I came out the door to help in his defense, he let down his guard for an instant. That was all Clarence needed to get in a nip and a slap. We don't get as many visitors as we used to before we had the geese. My wife thinks they should leave. Actually, everyone thinks they should leave. If I could find another home for them . . . a really, really good home, I would be okay with that. Except Monica, she needs to stay. I've planted apple trees.

Monica the Gentle Goose

Backwoods Peasant

My life's aspirations seem quaint to most. Maybe a little lacking in motivation or imagination.

Long-term planning has never been one of my strong suits. Possibly because I grew up in a household that moved on average every two years. Most of my life, I've flown by the seat of my pants . . . much to the dismay of my parents and the frustrated bewilderment of my long-suffering wife.

It's not that I didn't have goals. I wanted to live in the country. On a farm, where I could work from home, raise my own food, and be self-sufficient. I wanted my wife to be able to stay home if she wished. The two of us working together towards a common goal. Raising our children to be self-sufficient. But not just in the material sense. I envisioned our children growing up strong and confident in who they were as people, not needing material things to validate them as men or women. This, as it turns out, is more difficult than one can imagine.

We did buy a farm when we were young and our children were very small. It was perfect for what we wanted to accomplish. It had a small orchard as well as grape vines, gooseberry, and currant bushes, a quarter acre of asparagus, row upon row of raspberries, a chicken coop, and a small barn. The soil was so rich and workable and already over an acre was set up as a market garden. The 3-bedroom brick house was over one hundred and thirty-five years old and full of country charm. Which meant it needed lots of work. This was not a problem. As a young man two of my greatest assets were a strong back and a willingness to work harder than anyone else. Those two things seemed to compensate for my ignorance in farming. But not, as it turns out, a personality that was always looking over the fence at the next project, the next great adventure. Homesteading takes a strict dedication, long-term planning, and a laser beam focus for the job at hand. I was a dreamer.

After two and a half years, money was tight but things were progressing well. So well in fact, we thought we should share our wonderful family and lifestyle with someone less fortunate.

Foster kids were added to the mix. A brother and sister. Pre-teens. They were wards of the province. They could never be adopted and they could never go home. Their parents were alcoholics and abusive. Now we had six children between the ages of five and twelve and our house was too small. So, we bought a five bedroom, one-hundred-acre farm and moved everyone along. But it had already become clear, rather than being a positive influence in their lives, the level of dysfunction in their previous lives was causing havoc and dysfunction in our current lives.

After almost a year we admitted defeat and the children were placed in another home. We sold our farm and bought a smaller one. The most beautiful one of all. Fifty acres, with a four-bedroom brick home, a huge barn, a stream, and woods. Really, a perfect farm on so many levels. We raised chickens for meat and eggs, as well as rabbits, pigs, and cattle. We had a Jersey cow we milked daily and even made our own butter. But after all the moves and our failure in foster care, some of the magic seemed to be gone.

I have a picture from those early days, but I don't look at it often. It always makes me cry. I'm walking away with a feed bucket in my hand. My two sons are behind me and behind them are a few of our horses. By the facial expression on my oldest son's face, it was obvious he was talking to me. My head is half turned and I must have been answering him. It makes me sad only in that I was walking away, head only half turned. If I could change the picture, I would be bent down looking into his face, giving him my full attention. I was distracted in those days. Worried about money and things that seemed important at the time.

My wife and I did get to stay home and be with our kids every day. I always knew how fortunate we were. But of course, there never seemed to be enough time.

One of the things I did for income in those days was presentations in schools. We called it "The Roving Reptile Review." A live hands-on demonstration/presentation of exotic snakes, lizards, turtles and such.

My youngest daughter, Virginia, accompanied me one day when I drove to a school in Toronto. She was only eight years old and very shy. She assisted me as best she could, but was embarrassed to be in front of so many people. On the way home she was tired and fell asleep beside me. I remember looking over at her and being completely overwhelmed by how beautiful and perfect she was. And in some odd way, feeling undeserving of such an exquisite gift and responsibility.

Life has a way of making a thinking man humble. Our oldest daughter died several years ago, but I am very proud of her children. Our oldest son sustained a traumatic brain injury in a fall while rock climbing, but is strong and carries on with a determined zeal in spite of his disabilities. Our youngest daughter moved to South Korea to teach English without knowing the Korean language or anyone there.

Our youngest son is married with children of his own: a musician and artist of great talent.

They all credit farm life with their fondest memories. Their work ethic, their understanding of the natural world, their independent and strong personalities all grew along with the love we have for each other on those farms.

I'm back to homesteading on a much smaller scale. My ambition now is the same. I want to be a backwoods peasant. Making a life from the ability to coax grace and generosity from a piece of land. I would like to instill a desire in my grandchildren to understand the importance in helping something to grow. To nurture something, to help bring out the best in its being. Plant, animal, or child. In this, is great privilege, great responsibility, great rewards, and potential risks for great heartache. Even so . . . in this, is the greatest peace.

A Grandfather, A Granddaughter, A River

Most days are pretty good. Today was great! It's summertime and a Friday, sandwich me in the middle of that and it's a tasty day. My beautiful granddaughter is visiting and we like to ring every drop out of a day, so kayaking and a bike ride seemed to be our likely choices. We loaded up the boats and drove a short distance to the river. Of course, there was no conversation . . . she's fourteen and has an iPhone. I unloaded the kayaks and we dragged them down to the water. The river is low and there's not much of a current. There are a few puffy white clouds in a perfect "Carolina blue" sky. A slight breeze pushed some ripples across a calm glass-like surface and we slide off the sand and into the water with barely a whisper. She paddles out to the middle of the river, and I hug the shoreline looking for clues as to what lives here.

A water snake drops off a rock when I get too close and glides along beside me until it finds a crevice in the rocks of a cliff that has come down to meet the river bank. It poked its head up and I reached out with my paddle and stroked its neck. The snake slithered up the paddle but fell off when it came to the narrow handle. I called out to my granddaughter to come and look but she was now on the other side of the river and the snake would be long gone before she could get here. She had stopped paddling and I could see her head was in that familiar downward position checking her phone. The breath of a heavy sigh rushed past my lips and I wondered how I could tweak her interest in the beauty that surrounded us.

She started a Katy Perry fan page on Twitter; it takes a lot of her time. Then of course there's Snap Chat, Facebook, and returning all those texts. It's a full-time job being fourteen. I paddled further down the shoreline.

The constant hum of a hundred million insects, punctuated by the songs of an indigo bunting and a scarlet tanager set the sound track for this unfolding scene. The breeze picked up and the wind that blew through the leaves of a nearby stand of sycamores sounded like a hundred people standing in applause. A huge snapping turtle swam beneath my kayak, its neck stretched out a full eight inches. Carp slapped their tails against the surface and an osprey drifted lazily overhead. I looked for my granddaughter. She still had her phone in her hand, but now she was taking pictures.

We pulled our boats up on a sand bar and got out to explore. A killdeer tried getting our attention by running along the shoreline pretending it had a broken wing. I explained to my granddaughter that she had young hidden somewhere close by and was doing her best to lure us farther away. So, we followed her, letting her think she was doing her job. When we were far enough away, she quit her act and flew back to where she had stashed her babies. Bubbles popped up from beneath the sand and we dug down looking for mussels. There are bald eagles along the river, so when I saw a large bird soaring overhead, I said, "Is that an osprey or an eagle?"

"It's an osprey," she said. She was right.

We walked to our kayaks and paddled back up the river. A doe came down to the water's edge for a cool drink in the heat of our July afternoon. We watched her for a few moments, until she turned, stepped back into the woods, and disappeared like a ginger ghost.

A perfect summer's day on the New River in Virginia. I looked at my granddaughter and tried to imagine what she was thinking. Her life hasn't been easy. Her mother died five years ago next month. So, I try to cut her some slack when I feel a melancholy come over her and she gets quiet and a little unresponsive. Fourteen is a hard age regardless of your circumstances. Earlier today she asked me, "Do you think that people who don't believe in God go to Heaven?" Usually, I try to answer questions like that with more questions, designed to provoke independent and critical thought. After all, I question God every day. I think He likes it. But today, I told her what I really thought.

And now, here we are. In the great cathedral of the living God, having church. Real church.

Loving each other and everything created surrounding us. There is no greater gift.

She's fourteen and trying to decide what is real, and what will be important in her life. I already know. Today it's kayaking and bike riding with this ever so beautiful, intelligent young lady.

Unfinished Business

I was relaxing on the hammock the other day. I guess I was assessing our lives. My wife's and mine. I had a cold drink in my hand, the sun was setting, and I was feeling intimate with my surroundings. It's a piece of property we have worked closely with for over a decade.

Sometimes I feel fortunate and wonder what I ever did to deserve all this. Other times I don't fully understand how we have survived what life has thrown our way. Often, when I'm alone, I try to concentrate on the positive and do a mental inventory of everything I'm grateful for. The list is substantial. That's what I was doing this late afternoon.

The day was slowly trading places with the evening and the songs of birds were being replaced with the calls of crickets. Everything was peaceful, and I felt my spirit resting in a place of gratitude. But I was taken off guard with a sudden and overwhelming feeling that I was very far from home. I felt panicked, like I needed to return somewhere and take care of unfinished business.

I had a home once, that I loved. Maybe even more than the home I have now. But I was just a boy and had earned nothing. Of course, that's not entirely true. I had earned the respect and friendship of an old man. He was ten years old when the slaughter at Wounded Knee took place, and ninety-one years old when I met him. A "Holy Man" in the truest sense of the definition. Although that wasn't a claim he ever made, it was obvious to anyone that spent time with him. He was awarded the "Order of Canada Medal" for his work in ornithology. He wrote a book called *I live with Birds* and articles for the National Geographic. He understood that animals had emotions, and could feel love and loss at a time when science scoffed at the very notion. He had a small home in the woods surrounded by large aviaries. It was a bird sanctuary.

People sent him injured and rare birds from all over North America. He set the hollow bones of broken wings and legs, determined the exact formula to be fed to any number of baby birds, raised them up, or healed them, and released them into the wild to live as they were meant to live. All the while, showing the same level of care and respect to the life that now rested in his hands, be it sparrow or eagle.

Every day I made my way across the meadow, over the stream, and through the woods to his home. Every day he taught me something new. I met him when I was eleven years old and had to leave him when I was fifteen.

Four decades later, I sometimes awake from the same dream. All the birds are dead. I wasn't there to feed them.

It wasn't the place. It was him. He was my home.

My home now is where my wife is. Our children are adults, living too far away. My thoughts drifted to them and our own intimate tribe . . . our family. What a gift it was to have them as children, all to ourselves. We were our home then. A time so intense and wonderful. It passed too quickly, was over too soon. I realized then what I was feeling. I was very far from "that home." My kids will never be children again, and I . . . will never again be a young man. But I can still open a door and enter into a room where I hear my kids say . . . "Dad's home!" I still hear them as they come thundering up the stairs to greet me, still feel them in my arms as we roll around on the floor, feel their hair in my face as they kiss me, hear their laughter when I tickle them, and feel their weight on my back as they ride the "bucking bronco."

I guess there is no "unfinished business." If we are very fortunate, we will have had several "homes" in our lifetimes. Each one cradled in the arms of our minds and our hearts. Each one changing us from one person into someone else. Wiser, stronger, fuller . . . better.

Tag-Along

I turned nine years old during the summer of 1967. It was the first time I remember moving.

My father had been transferred to a small town in upstate New York. Clayton was a tourist town situated along the St. Lawrence River. The Thousand Island Bridge spanned the river and connected Canada and the United States. My father worked at the border, checking cars and their passengers for contraband.

In Ontario he worked at the Toronto airport where he had met people like Elvis Presley, the Beatles, and the Rolling Stones.

All the stars and celebrities would have to pass through customs coming off their flights. Sometimes he would come home with autographed hockey sticks from NHL players or hockey pucks. He liked the Beatles, but said the Rolling Stones smelled so bad he couldn't stand to be close to them. He thought Elvis was a "real gentleman."

The transfer to Clayton must have seemed boring by comparison. We moved in the summer, when school was out. There were no houses for rent, so we rented a cottage along the river. It was beautiful. I remember waking up very early one morning, before it was even light outside. I noticed my mother quietly sitting on the porch in the dark. I walked outside and stood beside her.

"What are you doing, Mom?" She turned her head and looked at me in a way that only a mother can.

"I'm listening," she said.

I turned and looked as the first hint of light was breaking through and strained to hear what she was hearing. Crickets, frogs, and the faint songs of birds just waking up.

"It's the sound of the night trading places with the day," she whispered. Her hand reached out and pulled me in close. "What are you doing up so early?"

I didn't know.

We stayed in that cottage for two weeks, then moved to another for a month, then another. When it became apparent there were no houses to rent, my father bought one. It was the biggest house I ever lived in. My two older sisters finally had their own rooms, a fireplace in the living room was my father's delight, and there was even a music room. My mother bought a used piano from the Catholic church and began taking lessons. Best of all, the house was one block from the river.

In September, I started school and was hoping to meet some new friends as it had been a lonely summer. However, I was from Canada, which meant I talked differently from the kids at school. The first thing I learned in fourth grade was that kids don't like "different."

"You're a weirdo. You talk weird."

Being Catholic, it was of course, a Catholic school. Almost all the teachers were nuns. The school was attached to the convent, and run with an iron hand by the "Mother Superior." A tiny wisp of a woman, no taller than an average fourth grader. In those days all the "sisters" wore the standard issue "habits." It made them look as though they walked on air.

From the day I walked into Sister Barbara's class, I knew two things. She loved me, and my classmates did not. Almost every day after school, I would walk down to the river. Some days I would watch the big ships pull in and fill up with coal. The sailors would come off the ship, stand around, smoke cigarettes, and curse. Other days, I would walk along the shore feeling sorry for myself. On one such day I had plopped myself down on a log, put my head in my hands, and was wondering if my life could get any worse. My father was always working, my mother was a teacher at a school in a neighboring town and sometimes didn't get home till after six. My sisters had no patience or time for their annoying little brother and I had no friends to explore this really cool river with. One of the benefits of being raised Catholic, was knowing that I could talk to Jesus anytime and he would hear me. I decided it was time Jesus and I had a talk. This was really too much for my nine-year-old heart to have to bear. Jesus needed to fix it . . . now! So, there I was, head in my hands, laying out all the reasons Jesus should feel as sorry for me as I did for myself.

"After all, Jesus, you know I'm gonna be a priest someday." At about the time I had gone from wallowing to drowning in my little pool of despair, I felt something wet and clammy touch my leg.

Startled, I looked up and saw a beagle puppy standing in front of me wagging his tail. He took a step forward, touched his nose on my leg again, then crouched down on his front legs and leapt back in the sand with a look on his face that seemed to ask: "What are you doing sitting there? Let's play!"

Play we did. He liked to chase sticks, but sniffing out anything that drew a breath as well as some things that had stopped breathing, seemed to be his passion. So, we walked along the shore stopping to investigate anything my new friend felt was worthy of a sniff. Which meant we stopped a lot. He was black, brown, and white with a tail that never stopped wagging. Even though he was deeply interested in where his nose was leading him, he responded to every noise or move I made. When the time came to head for home, he was beside me.

My parents had grown accustomed to their son bringing home the spoils of adventure. Usually in the form of snakes, frogs, turtles, or baby birds. Indeed, my mother encouraged my interest in anything nature related. While my father mostly played a disinterested role in my young life. I required copious amounts of stimulation and he was either unwilling or unable to accommodate my needs. We mostly seemed to avoid each other when we could. Even so, I knew him well enough to know what his reaction would be when I came home with a dog.

"I said no, and I mean it!"

He was addressing my mother; he rarely spoke to me directly.

"Every time that kid walks through the door, he has something alive in his hands! I'm tired of it! We don't need a dog!" My father stomped out of the room and she looked at me with the look that said there was nothing more she could do.

Sleep that night did not seem to be an option open for me. I kept getting up to look out my window, checking to see if the little silhouette of my new friend was still there. At some time, I must have drifted off because I woke in the morning to the sound of my father's voice scolding my mother.

"Oh, geez. Rita, that damn dog is still out there."

I threw my covers back, sat up, and looked out my window as my father was walking out to his car. The puppy came trotting up to my dad wagging his tail with a "Good Morning" greeting that should have melted his heart. He responded by throwing his hands in the air.

"Go home! Go on, git!"

The wagging tail shot instantly between his back legs and he ran away. My father got in his car and drove off. I got ready for school and came downstairs.

"You better eat something, sweetie." My mother was getting ready to leave the house herself.

"Not hungry," was the only reply I could muster up.

"Robbie, don't be upset with your father. What did you expect?"

What did I expect? What kind of question was that for a nine year old? I was at the mercy of what my father wanted. What I wanted, or liked seemed to have no relevance. What did I expect? Exactly what happened I suppose.

My sister, Nancy, walked in the kitchen. "That stupid dog is out on the front step."

I walked to school that morning accompanied by the sound of panting, and eight little toenails clicking on the sidewalk beside me. I had a grin on my face that I couldn't get rid of and every time I looked down at my friend, he looked like he was grinning too. When I got to school, I introduced him to Sister Barbara. She seemed to take a genuine interest in everything I did so I told her the story. She responded by heaping praises all over the little guy, while lovingly stroking his head.

That morning, I asked to use the bathroom twice before recess and each time I would sneak out the front door of school to see if he was still there. The third time I asked, Sister Barbara said no. I needed to finish my work. A few minutes later she left the room. When she came back, she bent down beside my desk and whispered, "He's still there, Robbie. Don't worry."

He was still there at lunch and was still waiting on the steps after school. We walked home to an uncertain fate.

My mother helped keep him hidden for the next couple of days, but my father came home early and saw him lying on the couch with me in the den watching tv. The dog had not gotten over this first encounter with my dad, and when my father appeared in the doorway, he immediately jumped off the couch and darted between his legs to a place of perceived safety.

There was no such place for me however.

"What did I say?" My father glared. I was panic stricken.

"What . . . did . . . I . . . say?" he repeated. The words drawn out this time for maximum effect, as though he was trying to contain a rage that was now boiling over to a point of non-containment. This was not good. He might have to kill me, I thought.

There was no defense, no words I could say to calm him, and no way I could get by him to flee to safety. I accepted my fate. Death was imminent.

"Bob!" my mother shrieked. "Calm down. It's okay, I told him he could bring him in here."

"What?!" My father couldn't believe what he was hearing.

"He follows him everywhere. A regular little tagalong. He won't leave."

"I can fix that!" my father huffed, and turned to find the offender. She reached out and grabbed him by the arm.

"No . . . you won't. He's not hurting anything by being here."

An intelligent man knows who holds the real power in a family. My mother gave the order and backed it up with a valid reason. That was all. I watched the anger fade from my father's eyes as the wisdom and tone of her words found their mark. He walked away humbled but not humiliated. My father loved my mother.

The biting cold of winter had rolled in and it was too frigid, for Tag-Along to be waiting outside all day at school. My mother would keep him inside until I left in the morning. Eventually he would have to go out to "conduct his business" and when he was done, he made a beeline for the school. Several times while walking by the principal's office on my way out for recess, Sister Phyllis would call out to me.

"Robbie, hold up. There's someone here for you."

I would look over and "Tag" would come tumbling out of her office.

Winters were colder back then. The St. Lawrence River would freeze over, and out would come the snowmobiles and fishing huts. Every year the town parked an old car out on the ice.

They held a lottery to see who could pick the day and hour that the car would fall through the melting ice in spring.

After that day, no one was allowed back on the river with snowmobiles. Within a week or so, you could hear the massive ice sheet cracking like gun fire as it broke up. Soon, huge chunks of ice the size of small islands would be floating down the river.

Father Peace was a new priest at St Mary's. He took me aside one day and asked if I would be interested in becoming an altar boy. This was somewhat of an honor for a young Catholic boy and I answered in the affirmative. I had to enter the side door of the church where the sacristy was. That was where the priests and altar boys changed into their robes before mass.

That room had another door that opened out onto the altar area of the church where the mass was performed. Father Peace was a young priest and all the altar boys liked and respected him.

The Monsignor was another matter. He was much older, long past retirement age and he had a speech impediment that made understanding him when he spoke to you a real chore. His homilies were a painful thing to endure and he was a little . . . shall we say . . . "cranky."

One Sunday morning, during the high point of the mass when the priest is busy with the holy ritual of turning the wine and bread or "Hosts" as they are called, into the actual body and blood of Jesus, Tag-Along walked out of the sacristy and onto the altar, looking for you know who.

Someone must have left the outside door open and he thought it was an invitation. A gasp erupted from the congregation, followed by muted giggles and uncomfortable squirming. I was standing beside the Monsignor assisting him in this most important and holy ritual when Tag spotted me. He trotted over and looked up at me with tail wagging. Red faced, I looked at the Monsignor who was obviously appalled by this unholy intrusion. He gave me "the look." I bent down and took "Satan" by the collar, led him down off the altar and out the side door.

Our church building was enormous. Almost cathedral like. At least it seemed that way to a young boy. It was summer time and, in those days, there was no air conditioning, so the huge front doors were left open so air could circulate. This, as it turns out, was not a good thing on this particular day. Back up on the altar now with the Monsignor I had a perfect view of a small beagle trotting down the center isle of St. Mary's church towards the altar. He climbed the steps and came dancing up to me as if to say, "Ha, found you." There was no fixing this. The nuns who were all fans of Tag-Along, always sat in the front pews. They could hold it together no longer.

Their hands covered their faces but you could see their shoulders bouncing up and down with laughter. In fact, their pews were bouncing. The rest of the congregation seemed equally amused and entertained. The Monsignor, however, was not. His face looked like a big red tomato as he motioned me to come closer. He mumbled something, his tongue flopping helplessly around in his mouth trying to form words that were coherent. I leaned in closer.

"TAKE YOUR DAMN DOG AND GO HOME."

The summer of '68 couldn't have been better. My father bought me a mustang bike. It had a banana seat and suicide handle bars. The kids in town had decided that I wasn't so weird after all. In fact, Tag-Along and I had become minor celebrities since word of our little dog and boy act in church hit the streets. I had friends now and we spent our summer riding bikes, building rafts, and going to free rock concerts on the river front. The town was a bustling little tourist trap, where the population more than tripled during the summer months. I saw for the first time that summer a young man with long hair. He played in a band called *The Lost and Found*. My mother took one look at him and said: "He looks like he's been lost alright, and someone found him in a ditch."

O'Brien's was a bar where all the hippies would hang out. They had bands on weekends and the sound of music and people enjoying themselves pulsated in my room till early morning. The bar was located directly behind our house, and I heard songs by the Doors, Vanilla Fudge, Cream, and others. They were cover bands, and sometimes they would play the same song a dozen times, but no one seemed to mind. People seemed happier then, more carefree. But maybe that was the outlook from a ten-year-old boy with no worries.

The summer of '69 my father was transferred back to Ontario and we rented a house along highway ten in Cooksville, not far from Lake Ontario. I started sixth grade at Saint Catherine's of Sienna and again was chastised by my peers for the way I talked. I had taken on an American accent and Americans were not well liked at this juncture in time. The Vietnam war was in full swing and Canadians were against it.

Every morning we would start our school day with "Current Events." Kids were asked to bring in newspaper stories cut out from local papers that we could read and discuss. Of course, the majority of articles were on the Vietnam war. I was eleven years old. What did I know? Mr. Hadel was anti-American and my sixth-grade teacher. He would make a point of centering me out and force me to defend my country's position. He seemed to delight in making a fool out of me and the rest of the class followed his example. It mattered little to me at the time because when I came home, I had the most honorable and loyal friend waiting on the other side of our front door.

We explored the fields, streams, and woods around our new home. One day while out hiking, I found a baby crow and brought him home to raise. Another addition to a steadily growing menagerie that included an alligator, rabbits, several cats, and a baby ground hog. Remember I told you . . . my father loved my mother.

One night I was awakened by hushed words and frantic activity in the house. I got up to see what was going on. My mother was crying.

"Robbie." She hesitated, trying to compose herself and choose her words.

"Your sister took Tag out for a walk and he got hit by a car out on the highway."

All the air had been sucked out of me, I felt dizzy.

"We took him to the vet and he said there was nothing he could do. He said that Tag was in a lot of pain and we should put him to sleep."

I felt hot tears running down my face. I really couldn't take in what she was saying.

"What? No! What happened? Where is he?"

"I couldn't do it, Robbie. I brought him home. I'm so sorry. Your sister is sick about it. It wasn't her fault."

She had fixed up a place for him in the den. Tag was lying on his side. His breathing was shallow and I could hear a gurgling in his chest. His eyes were closed, but when I touched his face, he opened his eyes and his tail thumped once. He couldn't pick his head up so I lay down beside him, my nose almost touching his. His breath was hot on my face, and every so often he would lick his mouth but his tongue was dry and white. His breathing would get faster, the gurgling would get louder, his little chest heaving up and down brought out soft whimpers that revealed the pain he was feeling. I wanted to stay with him until he died, but as it got later, my mother insisted I go to bed.

"I'll stay up with him. I'll wake you up if anything changes."

Lying in bed, I could make no sense of this event. It didn't even feel real somehow. Just a few yards away my best friend was dying. As a child you have no power. I didn't even have the authority to tell my mother that I was not going to bed, that I would stay with him. I was a nothing. I wished I was dead. It stands to reason then, when you reach the end of your own power, you have to rely on the power of someone greater. I bargained with God that night. There was something that I always felt God wanted me to do. Something just between the two of us. I told Him I would do it if He would save my friend.

I managed to fall asleep that night. But when I awoke in the morning and opened my eyes, the first thing I saw was the limp body of Tag-Along lying across the threshold of my bedroom doorway. Somehow during the night, he had managed to drag himself from the den to my room. He almost made it. Tag always slept at the foot of my bed. There was security in feeling him there with my toes, listening to the rhythm of his breathing, knowing he would be there when I woke up. I lay there looking at him. I wanted him to be alive so much, that at first, I thought I was hallucinating.

Did I just see him breathing? I flew out of bed! Tag? He lifted his head and his tail thumped the floor. He tried to get up but yelped out and lay back down. I laid down beside him and he licked my face. His tongue was wet and pink now, and I didn't hear any of those gurgling sounds in his chest. My mother came to the doorway. She had no words.

Tag recovered nicely, but since his recovery, always had a strange clicking sound in his chest when he ran. Something to remind me of my promise I suppose.

We moved from the house on the highway to a house in the country with a stream in the backyard and endless meadows and woods for us to explore. This was paradise for a twelve-year-old boy and his dog.

Inky, my pet crow, never knew a cage and would accompany us on our adventures. He was a member of our very exclusive club of curious explorers. The only problem we seemed to have, was that Inky wanted to be the boss. He certainly had the intellect for the job and the advantage of flight made it impossible for us to hide or run very far without being found. He had a great sense of humor as long as the joke was on someone else.

I had other pets as well. A very large and bossy goose named Waldo, who clashed with Inky on a daily basis, four chickens and a couple of ducks, a raccoon, pigeons, and a screech owl named Homer. The chickens and ducks were all raised together from hatchlings. The poor chickens didn't know what they were. I had to make a dramatic rescue one day after watching them follow the ducks into the stream. They just assumed they could swim, because, one by one they entered the water and flopped over on their sides and floated helplessly downstream towards a four-foot waterfall. The boy in me wanted to watch them go over but, my mother was watching and called out to me, "Robbie! Hurry, help those chickens before they get hurt!"

Some days my father would come home from work, fix himself a martini, grab the newspaper or a book and go sit in the backyard to relax. At least that would be his intention. Inky, however, found great pleasure in making sure that relaxing was something other people got to do. The peasants in his kingdom were there for his amusement.

"Oh, I see you have a drink . . . with ice cubes? Oh, I love the sound they make when I push your glass over.

"Oh, you're trying to read a newspaper? Don't mind me while I attempt to land on it and tear it to shreds."

"I see you're not wearing any shoes. I like toes. Or rather, the sound you make when I pinch them with my beak."

He was relentless.

Waldo was in love with Daisy, one of the ducks. If anyone got within a few feet of his beloved Daisy, all hell would break loose and the offending party would usually limp away bruised but wiser.

One afternoon I was keeping Inky entertained while my father and mother rested peacefully in the back yard. Waldo was strutting by with his little flock on their way to the stream for some swim time. Inky saw an opportunity.

I need to pause here to explain something to you, the reader. Inky owned the world. That is all. If you were in his world, taking up space, breathing his air, you were just going to have to pay a toll. The toll changed with his moods or his ideas about how things should be run on that particular day, or at any given moment. We never knew just how it would go down . . . we just knew it would.

We all watched as he swooped down, gliding low across the backyard. Waldo was always on guard waiting for a surprise attack. When you have eyes on the sides of your head, your peripheral vision is pretty good. But Inky was an expert in covert activities. He landed unseen behind the hemlock tree. A strategic position to be sure, as the unsuspecting group would have to pass by to get to the water. Waldo herded his little harem in front of him, stopping now and then to pull up a grassy snack. They waddled past my parents honking and quacking their salutations. I saw Inky's little black head dart out from behind the tree, his beady eyes and quick wit assessing the playing field. This was going to be ugly. About five feet from the tree, Waldo suddenly stopped and gave a warning honk to his ladies. I watched him looking around nervously. Apparently, he couldn't locate Inky. That was always a problem for everyone.

If you could see him, you were usually safer than when you couldn't. The tension was thick. Waldo took another couple of steps. Inky could not risk losing the target. It was a black blur that shot out from behind the tree. Waldo didn't have a chance. Inky had closed down tight on a beak full of goose tail feathers. Waldo jumped straight up in the air, his legs were already moving when he hit the ground, and he flapped his wings for a running take off. Inky didn't or couldn't let go, and was dragged along behind for over forty feet twisting, bouncing, and somersaulting.

When he finally was able to release his grip, he rolled in a most undignified manner another six feet. Apparently, this had not gone as planned. He was pretty shook up. But more than that, he was embarrassed. I never saw my father laugh so hard or for so long. I think my mother peed in her pants, because she ran for the house laughing hysterically clutching her lower extremities. Inky flew up into the hemlock tree where he spent the rest of the day sulking.

And, I'm certain . . . plotting his revenge.

Tag, Inky, and I had a relationship that for some reason seemed odd, and even difficult for others to understand. I had friends of course, but seemed to prefer the company of a crow and a dog. They were the co-conspirators of my youth and followed me everywhere. We explored the old barns and orchards, followed the stream until it emptied into the Credit River. And then we followed that. I brought a backpack with a lunch, made camp fires, and pretended I was a pioneer in uncharted lands like Daniel Boone. Tag was a wolf and Inky an eagle. Together we became intimate with every woods, stream, meadow, and valley within a couple of miles of our house. But every evening I was home in time to call the residents of "the shed" in and make sure all had food, water, and clean bedding before securing the door for the night. Inky found a roost somewhere in the woods and Tag slept on my bed.

Other than taking care of my animals, during the summer months I had virtually no responsibilities. When my chores were completed and if the weather was good, the three of us headed out to explore. We usually started by following the stream behind our house.

Inky and Tag always had their nose and beak in everything I was looking to study and were always ready to help conduct an inquiry. Talking to them like they were just two other people was normal to me. Whether it was the tone in my speech, body language, or the understanding that develops from spending hundreds of hours together, we seemed to have no trouble communicating.

One afternoon the three of us were busy lifting rocks and turning over logs to see who and what lived underneath. I rolled over a dead tree trunk lying by the stream bank, but before I could even see what was there, Inky had reached in and grabbed an exposed salamander. I scolded him and tried to get the poor creature away from certain torture and death. I picked up a colorful stone and made a fuss over it like it was something special, a real prize. That was usually enough to get Inky to drop whatever he had and come after what he then would perceive had more value.

"Oh, look what I have, Inky! Tag! Look at this!" I brought the stone to Tag so he could have a sniff. That was all it took. Inky dropped the salamander in the water and flew towards the new treasure. I let him snatch the stone from my fingers like he had stolen it away from me. He derived even more pleasure from an object if he thought you still wanted it. I pretended to try to grab it back and the game was on.

Unknown to us, an old man was watching our antics. He had been sitting on a rock just ten meters up stream enjoying the late afternoon summer sun and had no idea it would turn into a front row seat for a vaudeville comedy. I saw him first, which was highly unusual. Inky and Tag were always aware of anything out of the ordinary before me. So, I was quite startled to look up and see another human in our private world. There were no homes or farms close by, it was odd to encounter another person out here.

"You keep strange company, boy."

Even the sound of another person's voice seemed out of place here. This was our world, and I felt immediate concern about a door opening into our privacy. And if the truth has to be told, probably embarrassed I had been caught talking to animals.

Tag and Inky were surprised by the voice but quickly launched an investigation. Inky flew over to show the stranger his very special stone and Tag splashed across the stream with tail wagging, both introducing themselves in typical fashion. I was hesitant, but followed along behind my friends.

The man was old. That was obvious. He had a gaunt look, deep set eyes under a pair of unruly, wiry eyebrows, and a high forehead topped with thick but receding gray/white hair. His rather large, but straight nose was underlined by a small gray mustache that outlined a black and rose-colored pipe held firmly in place by pale thin lips. He looked frail and unsteady as he rose up to greet us from his perch on the rock. Black suspenders draped over a blue and black plaid shirt held up a very worn pair of bluish gray trousers, and most surprising to me, on his feet he wore bedroom slippers.

Tag had wasted no time giving him the once over, sniffing toes and waiting to be petted. Inky had already dropped his stone and was on the man's shoulder tugging at his suspenders by the time I was close enough for introductions.

The old man removed the pipe from his mouth. "Well, isn't he a corker?"

He didn't seem at all unnerved to have a crow on his shoulder hacking away at his clothing. That surprised me. I had never witnessed anyone so calm or unafraid of something that would seem to be so unnatural. He waggled a finger at Inky.

"Aren't you a little imp?"

Inky grabbed his finger gently, then let go. The man waggled again.

"You are a little imp."

Again, Inky grabbed his finger and let go.

"His name is Inky," I said.

The old man turned to look at me.

"And what's your name?"

"Robbie," I said as I looked down at the old man's slippers.

"And who's this?" he asked looking towards Tag-Along who had already satisfied his curiosity and moved on to sniff other things.

"That's Tag-Along," I said.

"Well, they are both suitable names." The old man looked at me again and I was instantly drawn into his eyes. They portrayed the most gentle expression of curiosity and kindness.

"My name's Roy, I live just through the woods there a bit."

"Really?" I said. "I never knew there was a house back in there."

I was surprised, because I thought I had explored this whole area. But, in truth I had never gone into that section of woods.

As it turned out, his name was Roy Ivor, a famous ornithologist. He invited us back to his house, which was little more than a small cottage in the woods, surrounded by huge aviaries that contained everything from blue jays to eagles. We sat on his front porch and talked as wild chickadees and nuthatches attempted to land on him and steal a treat from his breast pocket. It was where he always kept peanut chips for his friends. In no time we were talking like old friends. I found myself saying things out loud that I had never said to anyone else. He seemed to have a perfect understanding of my feelings about nature and my relationship with the natural world.

When he saw me along the stream bank with Inky and Tag-along, he must have recognized a kindred spirit immediately. From the first time we met our age difference seemed incidental.

Inky had wasted no time in setting up a perimeter, a no-fly zone. When he had successfully run off the hungry opportunists, he turned his attention to Tag-Along who was peacefully sleeping at my feet. A well-placed hammering with that "ice pick" we called a beak on Tag's head destroyed any hopes of a lazy nap. Inky had to be in control and the center of attention.

Mr. Ivor was amused, but thought it best if we left Inky at home for our next visit.

Over the next three years Mr. Ivor and I became close and I was privileged to have him as my mentor.

At ninety years old, he was still capable, but glad for my help. He complained of cataracts in his eyes and because of his failing sight, had trained himself to drag his feet so as not to risk stepping on any birds that were too tame to move out of the way as he made his rounds.

Morley was a very majestic-looking golden eagle that would sometimes accompany Roy on his almost half mile walks to the mailbox. He was sent to the sanctuary by some natives who had cut down a tree without noticing the nest. When the tree fell, his sibling was killed, and Morley's wing was so badly damaged that Roy was unable to help. Now they were friends. At first Morley looked at me with suspicion and even contempt. But I could see sadness in those piercing brown eyes.

This raptor should have been king of the skies, but instead, his left wing hung low and he walked clumsily where he needed to. By fall, Morley was taking meat from my hand and following me around his huge aviary as I cleaned and changed his water. What a privilege it was to win the trust of such a magnificent soul.

There were hundreds of birds there. Some being studied, others being treated for various wounds or ailments. In the spring so many baby birds were brought in, that by the time we finished feeding them all, it was time to start again. This went on from first light till it was dark. A wild red-tailed hawk that Roy had somehow befriended also came on a daily basis to be fed.

Baby screech owls, hawks, herons, robins—nothing was turned away and everyone was treated with the same level of respect and care.

At the end of the day, we would sit out on the porch, Roy would smoke his pipe and tell me stories from his past until mosquitoes drove us in the house. A cantankerous Steller's jay, who adored Roy, had the run of his place. He was always hiding Roy's pens and generally making a nuisance of himself. Like all corvids she was highly intelligent and required copious amounts of stimulation. I was never able to win her over. Roy belonged to her, and I was seen as competition.

Another school year was starting, and another new school to attend. St. Martins had 800 kids and 60% of them were girls. I was in seventh grade now and we had started to notice each other. I made quite an impression the first day, when the bus came to pick me up at the end of our very long driveway. You couldn't see the house from the road because it sat back in the woods. But there I was, walking to the bus with a dog at my side and a crow on my shoulder. Of course, Inky felt it his right, even his duty to make a thorough inspection of the bus and its passengers and became enraged when I wouldn't let him come aboard. He followed the bus for a mile down the road flying even with the windows still looking for a way in. My peers were impressed and gave me a new name "Robird LaCrow."

Every day after school and every weekend I made my way across the meadow over the stream and through the woods to Roy's and every day I learned something new. There was something about this man. So calm and gentle. I would watch him; the way he handled an injured or sick bird. Sometimes, I felt like I was in the company of a "Holy Man." More so than any priest or Nun or any religious person I had known. This was real to me and it resonated in a way that led me to believe that being here was the most important thing in the world.

It was a few days after Christmas. I was up early to do my own chores then make my way through the deep snow to Roy's. I had some time off from school for the winter break, and was looking

162

forward to time I could spend there. I came in the house to grab a quick breakfast before heading out. My father was standing at the doorway going into the kitchen with a look on his face that I had never seen before. My mother came up and stood beside him. They looked at me and I knew something terrible had happened.

"I don't think you should go to Mr. Ivor's today, Robbie." My father was serious.

"Why . . . what's . . ."

"It was just on the news . . . his house burned down early this morning."

"What!? I have to go!" I ran out the door and through the back yard. Somewhere I heard my mother's voice call out, "Wait, I'll drive you."

But I couldn't wait, I couldn't stop, I had to run. I don't know if I was running away from something or running to something. It didn't matter; I just had to run.

Soon, I was standing in front of a stone fireplace surrounded by a seething, hissing mound of ash. White smoke and steam rising from what was left of my friend's home. The fire trucks had gone, but there were people milling about. Roy Ivor's Winding Lane Bird Sanctuary was well known in the area. Roy Ivor was highly regarded as Canada's foremost ornithologist and the curious were arriving.

I was somehow not a part of this scene. People were talking, but I didn't hear them. I felt like people couldn't see me. This dream belonged to someone else. I was here against my will.

Then I noticed the dead birds in the surrounding cages. Overcome by smoke, or maybe the heat of the fire, or worse.

I imagined them panicked, thrashing around, flying against the wire trying to get free. I found myself standing over the body of Morley, watching to see if he were breathing. I knelt down and put my hands on him to see if I could feel him breathing, or maybe a heartbeat. He was as beautiful in death, as he was in life. Someone touched my shoulder, but I didn't need to look, I knew who it was.

"Is Roy dead?"

Bernice Inman had been helping Mr. Ivor at the sanctuary for years. They were close friends. She came often, but we always seemed to be in each other's way. She tolerated me, but I could tell she would be happier if I wasn't there as much.

"No, Robbie, he's gonna be okay. He's at the hospital."

She pulled me up, and taking my face in her hands, looked into my eyes. The confusion fell away and was replaced by an overwhelming sadness. I burst out crying, great heaving sobs that came from a foreign place in me. There was no compass to guide me away from these feelings. I had never been here before. And neither had she. I was pulled into her chest, as if she could no longer bear looking at me. Her chest heaved hard and from somewhere deep inside, the sound of her breaking heart. We bonded in that moment of total despair. Holding each other, because we didn't know what else to do, until we were exhausted from crying. People were staring, but we didn't care. This pain had to excised in the most primal way and we were not capable of stopping until it stopped itself.

When I got to the hospital, Roy was lying in bed with bandages over his eyes because they were injured from the smoke. He was also being treated for frostbite and exposure as well as shock.

He told me that when he got out of bed, he noticed a light on in the living room. When he went to investigate, he saw a fire. He went to the kitchen to get a bucket of water, but by the time it was full, the whole living room was ablaze. He tried to release some of the birds from their cages but the smoke was too thick and the fire too hot, so he stumbled out to the porch where he listened to the screams of the birds and the crackling of dry wood.

"I can't ever go back there." His voice was weak and it kind of trailed off. "I guess I'm done."

Roy spent his ninety-first birthday in the hospital and then moved in with a nephew.

Meanwhile the whole community rallied around this event. Tens of thousands of dollars were raised through donations from all over the country. If Mr. Ivor had the will to rebuild and carry on, then he had all the help he would need. I knew he would. A house trailer was purchased and moved onto the property. Cages were rebuilt and birds continued to come that needed care. Mr. Ivor still had a purpose and we were busier than ever.

Like everyone else, my middle school years were a mixture of ecstasy and despair. But, when I came home from school, I was in the company of parents that loved me and each other, older sisters that were only as mean to me as I deserved, a house in the most beautiful natural surroundings imaginable, and bonds with animal friends that could not be comprehended by the average person. Thinking back now to those days seems like a dream. I am often left wondering what kind of man I would be today if we could have stayed there until I left for college.

When the word came down to me that we were once again moving back to the States, I felt sick.

Three short years in paradise was not long enough. Tag-Along, Inky, and a couple of cats could come, the rest I had to find homes for. Not only was this unfair, it was impossible. I couldn't give away my friends. They only knew me. Who would have the patience for my raccoon? I couldn't separate the goose, ducks, and chickens. Someone would have to take all of them.

Rabbits, guinea pigs, pigeons—the list went on and on.

Angry, hopeless, confused. These were words I could use to describe how I was feeling. There are no words to describe some emotions. We can feel them but we can't speak them.

Events change us from one person into someone else and we never fully realize how we have become who we are.

I had to assess the damages. Inky was now in a small cage in the laundry room of our new house. When I stepped out of the house with Tag he had to be on a leash because in any direction I looked, I saw houses, people, pavement, and cars. It was a smelly, busy factory town in upstate New York. This is where I would start high school.

My father was still stationed in Canada because at the last minute they decided they still needed him there. My mother was on her own for the next nine months. Perfect! She would be powerless while I transformed myself into a surly, self-absorbed, bitter teenager. I couldn't have my old life, so, I would create a new one.

Spending some time here, writing details of a young man who chose to ignore the moral standards and integrity that he was raised with, in order to waste the gift of time that was given him would doubtless interest some. In order to write about it, I would first have to relive it. I choose not to. Besides, these same tired stories have been told a thousand times by a thousand fools like myself.

They do nothing to honor the memory of my friends and serve only to sensationalize events best left forgotten. It is enough to say that before I turned eighteen, I was barely in school, had not been home for months, and was living with a young woman a couple of years older than me. I was in love. We were planning to move to South Carolina in a few weeks to start a new life.

My mother called one day to tell me that they had been transferred back to Canada. She knew better than to ask if I wanted to come. They had tried hard, even rented an older farm house in the country where I could have some space. But it was too late. My transformation was complete. I didn't stay.

"I found a home for Inky," she said. "A woman in Syracuse has a bird sanctuary there and thinks she can handle him."

I didn't know what to say.

"I couldn't find a home for Tag; you know he's had some health issues and I didn't want to put that on anyone."

I knew what was coming.

"Robbie, I had Tag put to sleep. I thought maybe you'd want to come over and say goodbye before we . . ."She hesitated; her voice faltered.

"Or maybe you want bury him?"

She wasn't calling to give me this news to hurt me. I had put her through a lot in the last couple of years and she had taken good care of Tag and Inky. She did it because she loved me, and knew how much they meant to me. She loved them as well. Because I was selfish, I never gave much thought to how the move here had affected her. She loved living in that paradise as much as I did. I remember her crying when we left, but I was too angry then to care.

She came to pick me up and we drove out to the farm in silence.

"He's in a box in the old milk house."

We got out of the car and she walked me to the door, but didn't go in. She turned around and went into the house. Beside the house, I saw the large aviary I had built for Inky. It was empty. I saw the box in the corner, walked over, and sat down beside it. I didn't look in. The cement floor was cold and for an instant I hated my mother. I saw my reflection in the window and hated that person as well. I didn't know who I was anymore and had forgotten the person I meant to be.

I looked in the box. He was curled up in a ball like he was sleeping and looked older than I remembered. He had a lot of white on his face. I reached in and pulled him out of the box and laid him across my legs. I stroked his little head and was so ashamed. I would have asked God for a miracle, but it had been so long since we spoke, I didn't know how. Besides I hadn't kept my promise.

I don't remember burying my friend, but I know I did, because years later my mother told me the saddest thing she ever had to witness, was looking out the window and seeing Tag in my arms as I walked with him out to the woods.

There are many things having a dog in your life can teach you. Mostly it teaches you what unconditional love really looks like. Tag never had to forgive me for anything I did because he never saw anything in me that needed forgiving. I think I have learned more about who God really is through the animals that have been placed in my life than I have through church or studying the Bible or listening to some learned theologian. I have had the gift of friendship with many dogs over the years and each one in some way has been a "salvation experience."

God's love must be unconditional as well. If that is hard for some to understand, maybe they need to get a dog. As for me, I strive to be the man my dog thinks I am. What higher standard can there be?

Robert and Inky

About the Author

Robert La Combe is an author and naturalist who lives in the Blue Ridge mountains of Virginia with his wife and an ever-changing menagerie of domestic and wild animals.

If you have enjoyed this book, you can write a review on Amazon.com.
Search for the title, click on *Customer Reviews*, then click *Write a Customer Review*.

Honest reviews will help other readers find me.

If you wish to contact the author, send an e-mail at woodlandsofivor@gmail.com